RARE BIRDS

A Look at the Baltimore Orioles from A to Z

By Chris Colston

ADDAX
PUBLISHING
GROUP

Lenexa, Kansas

Published by Addax Publishing Group
Copyright © 1998 by Chris Colston
Designed by Anonymouse Graphics and Printing
Illustrations by Mike Ricigliano
Photos courtesy Jerry Wachter

Distributed to the trade by Andrews McMeel Publishing
4520 Main Street, Kansas City, Missouri 64111

Printed in the United States of America
1 3 5 7 9 10 8 6 4 2

Library of Congress Cataloging-in-Publication Data

Colston, Chris.
    Rare birds : a look at the Baltimore Orioles from A to Z by
Chris Colston.
        P. cm.
    ISBN 1-886110-42-5
    1. Baltimore Orioles (Baseball team)--Miscellanea.   I. Title.
GV875.B2C65   1998   98-15954
796.357'64'097526--dc21   CIP

Dedication

For Melanie

Table of Contents

Acknowledgements

I owe thanks to many people for helping make this book possible. Addax Publisher Bob Snodgrass, of course, who agreed to take me on even though I had only one other book under my belt; freelance writer Roland Lazenby, who suggested my name to Bob in the first place; and freelance writer Mike Ashley, who afforded me my first newspaper job in 1983. He left as editor of the *New Castle (Va.) Record* to take a post with a local university, opening the door for me.

I also want to thank my bosses at *Baseball Weekly*–publisher Keith Cutler, executive editor Lee Ivory and deputy editor/operations Gary Kicinski– for giving me the go-ahead for this project; Baltimore Orioles assistant public relations director Bill Stetka, who offered insight and provided me with a wealth of stories; *Baseball Weekly* writer Bill Koenig, who was particularly helpful in my research and whose prose contributed some of the better anecdotes; *Baseball Weekly* editor Paul White and staff writers Tim Wendel, Deron Snyder and Pete Williams for their contributions; *Baseball Weekly* deputy editor Tim McQuay, an avowed Orioles fan who gave me perspective; freelance writer Louis Berney; Scott Zucker; Tom Suder; Wally Orlinksy and www.baltimorenews.com, whose Website proved valuable in my research; and my editor, Brad Breon.

Special thanks go out to *Portland Oregonian/Baseball Weekly* columnist John Hunt. Whithout him, I would not have been in position to write this book.

I especially want to thank my brother, Steve, for his invaluable suggestions and input; and my parents, Jim and Jo, for all the love and support they've given me throughout my life. Mostly I want to thank Melanie Kirsch. Without her encouragement, understanding, patience and good sense I never would have completed this book.

Chris Colston
March 1998

BATTING PRACTICE

"Bird Bird Bird, Bird is the word." – Trashmen, 1964

Perhaps you're a hardworking, honest person. You don't use office stamps for personal mail, you say "excuse me" after belching and you use your turn signal when changing lanes. But if you're holding this book in your hands, chances are that when it comes to getting that free pair of Baltimore Orioles tickets when the boss is away on vacation, you're elbowing old Mrs. Esefski into the water cooler, baby.

No? Not sure you're a diehard Orioles fan? Then maybe you should answer a couple of questions.

Did you shed a tear the night of Sept. 6, 1995? For your birthday, do you ask for a cake with black-and-orange icing? Is your favorite meal a hot dog, peanuts and a Natty Bo? Did your family give you vintage Boog Powell baseball cards for Christmas, while you privately prayed for box seats by third base at Camden Yards? Do you take vacation only when the Orioles go on an extended road trip?

Is your favorite article of clothing a goofy floppy hat you got for free at Orioles Floppy Hat Night? Do you own two MasterCards, because you had to get both the Cal Ripken version AND the one with Camden Yards on it? And did you go into a deep blue funk when broadcaster Jon Miller left for San Francisco?

If you answered "yes" to one or more of the previous questions, then you're hooked. You're a lifetime Orioles fan, like it or not. This book is for you.

What you'll find in these following pages is the lighter side of major league baseball in Baltimore. Inning by inning, we'll take you through the Orioles world: The frenzied fans, the beautiful ballparks, Earl, the legacy of pitching excellence, Cal and his amazing streak, past heroes such as Brooks and Frank and Boog, the wacky personalities and, of course, the World Series memories.

Read on, and enjoy.

	1	2	3	4	5	6	7	8	9	F
Visitor	0									
Orioles	1									

FIRST INNING
The Fans

"The fans are the people who keep you in town. The owner and the general manager don't do it. If the fans stop coming . . ."
– Former Baltimore Orioles manager Earl Weaver, who would rather not finish the sentence.

Whether you're a waterman from the shore or a downtown suit, a diner waitress or a high-powered attorney, attending a Baltimore Orioles game has always been about having a good time.

From the old days at Memorial Stadium to today's gleaming Oriole Park at Camden Yards, following the O's has been a celebration of sights, sounds, smells, tastes and touches. In the old days, fans parked along neighborhood streets, breathed in the aroma of freshly-cut grass, picked up a bag of roasted peanuts from an outside vendor and located a paint-chipped seat low in the upper deck at Memorial. Today, they might down a plate of garlic-and-butter mussels at Bertha's in Fells Point, take the water taxi to Camden and sit in a reserved seat because the game's a sellout. Around the fourth inning they might stroll down to Boog's for some pit-cooked barbecue, grab a microbrew and hang out over the center field railing, hurling good-natured insults at the opposing team's bullpen.

From marveling at Brooks and Cal at the hot corner; from

listening to the legendary play-by-play work of Chuck Thompson, the stellar Jon Miller, and now Fred Manfra, through a transistor radio ear piece; from emphasizing the O! in the pregame Star Spangled Banner to whooping it up to the late John Denver's "Thank God I'm A Country Boy" during the seventh-inning stretch, attending an O's game has always been a special experience.

A special experience — for special fans. In 1988 the "Woes" lost twenty-three of their first twenty-four games, including an

Boog Powell is still a fan favorite in Baltimore. Maybe it's the barbecue.

0-21 start. But they came home to a capacity crowd of 52,000.

On the final day of the 1982 season, on what was supposed to be Earl Weaver's final day in an Orioles uniform, Baltimore could have won the division with a victory. Although the Milwaukee Brewers prevailed that afternoon, O's fans stood and applauded Weaver long after the game was over.

These days, Baltimore fans are considered the best in baseball. And that's not some partisan opinion; it's the opinion of major leaguers themselves. A *Baseball Weekly* survey of 249 major league players revealed that O's fans are No. 1.

Every one of the 131 American League players polled rated Baltimore fans as either "very good" or "good." A whopping 81% of American League players polled rated them as "very good."

"They are in tune with the home team as well as the visiting team," Kansas City Royals closer Jeff Montgomery told *Baseball Weekly's* Bill Koenig. "They're very aware of not only the home team, but the visitor's statistics and history."

Wrote Koenig: "It was a sentiment echoed over and over. Players continually used words such as 'classy' and 'knowledgeable' to describe spectators at Camden Yards."

Said pitcher Aaron Sele, "They cheer a great play, even if the visiting team makes it."

The city loves its Orioles and the Orioles love the city. In the winters from 1967-77, no fewer than 16 Orioles and their families lived in Baltimore in the offseason. Popular Brady Anderson lives in the Inner Harbor during the season and often dons his Rollerblades and skates to work. He whizzes by fans who are oblivious that their hero was within back-slapping distance.

THE DAY IT BECAME COOL TO WATCH THE O'S: There wasn't always a love affair between Baltimore and the Orioles. Through the 1950s, the 1960s, and most of the 1970s, the National Football League's Colts were No. 1 in the hearts of Baltimoreans. Even though the O's had a following, Memorial Stadium was rarely sold out. But that began to change June 22, 1979, the night that helped transform Baltimore into a Baseball Town.

That was the year the O's radio rights switched from old, staunch megawatt station WBAL to WFBR, a more hip station featuring shock-jock deejay Johnny Walker. Chuck Thompson and Bill O'Donnell were still the club's announcers, but after the switch they started bringing different personalities into their radio booth.

Orioles assistant public relations director Bill Stetka was a sportswriter for Baltimore's *News-American* at the time, but on this warm summer evening a wedding (not his own) kept him from being at the game against Detroit. Instead he snuck out to his car to hear the broadcast. The late Charley Eckman was the night's celebrity guest. It was late in the game, and Doug DeCinces was at bat with Baltimore trailing. DeCinces connected, and O'Donnell, a classic-style announcer out of Syracuse who didn't get excited easily, began his call: "There's a drive deep to left …"

Eckman, an animated sort who had worked as an NBA official, NBA head coach, ACC official and sportscaster in his career, was in the background. "You could hear him screaming, 'Go on! Get out of here! Get out!' And as his voice rose, so did O'Donnell's," Stetka said. "Eckman was getting even O'Donnell excited, which I thought would never happen."

From then on, the broadcasts became livelier. Outfielder John Lowenstein made up T-shirts reading "Tonight, Let It Be Lowenstein," based on the popular Lowenbrau television commercials being broadcast at the time, and gave them out in the clubhouse (a marketing company later came in and sold them to the public).

"All that, along with that whole Wild Bill Hagy thing, made it COOL to go to baseball games," Stetka said. "It was a date/fun thing. It became a fun place to go for college kids, who could get in for $2.50."

Ah, Hagy. Perhaps no fan typified Baltimore and its blue-collar love of the O's better than Wild Bill, a city cab driver who for years led stadium-wide cheers from Section 34. With his big cowboy hat, long hair, pot-belly and thick arms waving, Hagy showed everybody how much fun being an Orioles fan could be.

WILD BILL HAGY: Tom D'Antoni, who produced the first national story on Hagy and Section 34 for Channel 13's Evening Magazine in 1979, was as familiar with him as anybody. He used to sit there with Hagy and a cast of others: Crazy Glenn, who

Wild Bill Hagy: He was an "L" of a fan.

would hit himself in the head with a cowbell during rallies; The Animal, who would celebrate a win by ripping the backs off of seats; Neil and Foudos who, armed with peanuts, had the pinpoint control of a Scott McGregor; the (late) Spaceman, Airplane Jane, Nurse Pat and Eddie Munster.

But Hagy was the star. "He was the best thing to happen to Oriole baseball since Brooks and Earl," D'Antoni said in a story in the sports section of www.baltimorenews.com.

"Come to Section 34 and watch the Orioles score and score!" Hagy used to say. And perhaps they scored more often because of him. Elrod Hendricks once told D'Antoni, "Bill really gets things going. Sometimes when we're down, some of the guys in the dugout would look up there and give him some of his same signs, and he'd get up and do the O-R-I-O-L-E-S and get the guys in the dugout going. He kind of got the adrenaline flowing."

Catcher Rick Dempsey usually urged Hagy on to do his alphabet bit, an act he ripped off from Len "The Big Wheel" Burrier, who had been physically spelling out C-O-L-T-S for years. We're talking about actually forming the letters with your body here. Sesame Street in 3-D.

"The Wheel's style, however, like football, was more aggressive," D'Antoni said. "Bill's was, well, slowed down by the pace of baseball and beer."

It wouldn't take long to get Hagy going; usually the bottom of the first inning, after his first cold one. He'd go to the top of the ramp, turn and face the section and wave his arms around, bellowing, "Are you ready?"

"The residents of Section 34 would answer with a resounding, 'Ooooooooooooooh we!!!' And from all over Memorial Stadium the 'O's' would begin," D'Antoni said. "And they wouldn't stop until Bill lowered his arms and hitched up his cutoffs.

"There would be a couple seconds of silence while the section re-filled its lungs. Then, he'd say, 'Let's hear it from the back row-ho-ho-ho-ho!!!!'"

Then Hagy would raise his arms over his head, forming an O, and the ballpark would explode. Then the R, with his right arm forming the curl, his right leg the stick of the letter. The I.

And the Orioles underneath Hagy aren't even worried about the dugout roof collapsing!

Another O. An L (that one was easy). An E (not so easy). Finally the S, of course. Then he'd end with both arms spread, fists clenched as the stadium rocked. It was glorious. So glorious, in fact, that Hagy would turn to face the rest of the stadium and do it all over again.

Hagy was no one-trick pony, though. "When the Orioles needed a run or two, and it looked like a rally was in order, Bill would stand up and wave his hat in a circle over his head," D'Antoni said. "The section would begin long and loud, 'Ooooooooooo oooooowe!!!' And the rest of the stadium would pick it up. It was quite a sight from another part of the stadium, to look up there and see hundreds of fans waving their hats and yelling."

Hagy's antics were a Memorial Stadium ritual, but it wasn't the only tradition in Section 34. "Every game, at least once a game, when Ken Singleton came to bat, Bill led us in, 'Come on Ken...put it in the bullpen!' and we'd point to the visitors bullpen in right," D'Antoni said. "When John Lowenstein came up, it was, 'C'mon Lowenstein, hit the Busch Beer sign!'

"When Al Bumbry came up, it was, 'C'mon Al, hit a home run now!' And we'd point to right field on the words 'home run.' When Lee May came up we all stood up and yelled, 'Leeeeeeee Maaaaaaaaaaaaaay!!!' as loud as we could, for as long as we could. It was quite primal. And it felt good."

Section 34 became more than a place to watch baseball. It became the neighborhood corner tavern. There were the regulars, there were the one-time visitors; there were those there to watch the game, there were those there to meet people. But instead of the game being on TV, it was live in front of them.

"The place was like a neighborhood," D'Antoni said. "The regulars sat in the same seats. People met, became couples, broke up or got married and had kids. People moved out to other sections. Some regulars who sat there for years never even talked to other regulars who sat there for years. A neighborhood.

"I had always sat behind home plate in the upper deck, pretty much since I went to my first game in 1954, but from the first time I sat in Section 34 in 1979 until the final tearful game at

Memorial, I just never wanted to sit anywhere else. It was an 81-game party every year."

Hagy and D'Antoni chose Section 34 because, first of all, it was general admission, and secondly, there was a men's room at the bottom of the ramp.

Was there rowdy behavior?

"Sure," D'Antoni said, "but nobody from Section 34 climbed up the right field foul pole."

Were there fights?

"No more than in the rest of the stadium," D'Antoni said.

Mainly, they just wanted to go to the ballgame, sit, have a few beers and talk baseball, and help pump up the other fans – and maybe even the team – "with some inspired screaming."

"It was fun. Rowdy, inebriated, sloppy fun," D'Antoni said. "It was a great time to be an Orioles fan."

Sadly, the rowdiness of Hagy and his cohorts hasn't transferred to glitzy Camden Yards. Hagy no longer goes to games. "Nobody's ever properly thanked Bill Hagy for helping to turn the quietest ballpark in the majors to the loudest," D'Antoni said. "I will. And if he should show up at Camden and begin waving his big old arms in the air, I'll be the first to start yelling, 'O!' "

	1	2	3	4	5	6	7	8	9	F
Visitor	0	0								
Orioles	1	1								

SECOND INNING

The Ballparks

"Camden Yards has turned downtown Baltimore into a celebration of baseball 81 days a year." – Karen Hucks, Tacoma News-Tribune.

Many fans thought Memorial Stadium was a dump; even former Orioles announcer Jon Miller complained, since he often found his view from his tiny, antiquated broadcast booth blocked by the visiting television crew.

But for the denizens of Section 34 and others, it was a house full of character. Sure, it had rats in the tarpaulin, but it also had a tomato garden beyond the outfield fence. The locker rooms might have been cramped, but many nights players used to hang out there, playing cards, smoking cigars, drinking beer and talking baseball into the wee hours of the night.

Thankfully, those rats stayed out of the clubhouse. "They were huge," Elrod Hendricks told author Peter Richmond in *Ballpark.* "One night, in the bullpen, Tippy Martinez was leaning against the fence looking in at the game, and this rat just walked across his feet. He turned to me and said, 'Was that a cat?' I said, 'No, that was a rat.'"

Before games the rats would hide in the tarp, and when fans would spill popcorn, they would come out. When it rained and the tarp was rolled out, they'd go in the drain. "That's why there were so many stray cats out in the bullpen," Hendricks told Richmond.

Memorial Stadium: A Memorable venue.

"They'd keep the rat population down."

But the rats knew better than to mess around in the Memorial Stadium tomato patch.

EARL SAYS TOMATO, PAT SAYS ...: Then-Orioles manager Earl Weaver and stadium groundskeeper Pat Satarone had known each other a long time. Satarone was into the whole dirt-and-gardening thing, so he and Weaver decided to have a friendly competition to see who could grow the best tomatoes. They created a tomato patch in a grounds-crew area down the left field line, where the outfield wall and the third-base stands met. They put stakes against the wall, which was out of play, and grew the tomatoes there until Weaver retired.

A PAIN IN THE GRASS: Memorial Stadium was a down-and-dirty kind of ballpark. One night vandals broke into Memorial Stadium before a game with the Chicago White Sox, and in the grassy crook of the infield at second base had spray-painted "Sox Sux." The resourceful Orioles grounds crew couldn't eradicate the handiwork by game time, so they spray-painted over the top of the "U" and turned it into an "O." So it read "Sox Sox."

GOODBYE, OLD FRIEND: As dingy as the place might have been, Memorial Stadium had one of the grandest good-byes in sporting history.

"The last game there was the most emotional moment I've ever seen in baseball and one of the greatest things I've ever seen in my life," said *Baseball Weekly* senior writer Bill Koenig. "It was like "Field of Dreams." People knew the club was going to do something special after the game, but nobody knew quite what.

"When the game was over, there were some ceremonies, then Brooks Robinson first took the field. He had on his old jersey and trotted out to third base, very ghost-like, and started kicking the dirt around the bag. Then Frank Robinson jogged out to right field, then Boog Powell to first, and Jim Palmer to the mound. This very dramatic music was playing over the loudspeakers, and more and more players came out – all of the Orioles who had

Camden Yards: A little bit of heaven here on earth.

played at Memorial Stadium went out and took their positions on the field. Finally, Cal Ripken came out, and then Earl."

But the Orioles didn't just introduce the big names. Even guys who had just one special moment in the spotlight trotted out. John "Tonight, Let it Be" Lowenstein and Gary Roenicke came out in tandem. Infielder Len Sakata came out to stand with the catchers, since his biggest moment was a three-run homer hit while filling in behind the plate.

"The people in the stands were just bawling, crying their eyes out," Koenig said. "It was an incredible surge of emotion."

It's easy to understand why. To a baseball fan, when a player's career is over, it's as if he dies. Simon and Garfunkel were on to something with their 1968 hit Mrs.Robinson and its famous line, "Where have you gone, Joe DiMaggio/our nation turns its lonely eyes to you." So when a player comes back in uniform, it's as if he has risen from the dead.

And it reminded everyone that these players had returned to pay homage to the place they had played all those years. Memorial Stadium wasn't pretty, but it was where many Orioles fans grew up. "Architecturally, it didn't have the best sight lines," said Stetka, who grew up in Baltimore. "But it was ours."

Longtime Orioles fan John Hunt, who writes a national fantasy baseball column for *Baseball Weekly*, says the aura of the farewell grows as time goes by. "Memorial Stadium was, well, a dump," he said. "It was a little bit of like, 'good riddance.' And everybody knew how good Camden was going to be, so they were looking forward to that.

"But the crowds were rowdier at Memorial, and the crab cakes were better than they are in Camden. They were only like $1.50 and came with saltines. You stuck the cake between the saltines and ate it like a little sandwich."

DYNAMIC NEW DIGS: After the tearful good-bye, the team moved into Oriole Park at Camden Yards, baseball's first throwback-style ballpark, on April 6, 1992. Only 12 minutes west by foot from the city's Inner Harbor and only two blocks from the birthplace of baseball's most legendary hero, Babe Ruth, the ballpark was constructed with steel – not concrete – trusses. An arched brick facade, asymmetrical playing field, and the generous use of classic green for the seats and fences gave the place a timeless feel. And the architectural design of the light stanchions and upper deck roof paid homage to the site's railroad history.

Although die-hards loved Memorial, they nevertheless embraced their new home.

"I grèw up in a row home in northeast Baltimore," Stetka said. "We had no air-conditioning, no dishwasher, a small backyard and we all shared a bathroom. When I was a teenager we moved to the suburbs and I had my own room, central air, a dishwasher, a driveway and more than one bathroom. I still go by and visit the old row house and revel in all the fond memories. But I don't want to move back there."

Ten Best Things about Camden Yards

10. Little door the grounds crew uses to get in their field-level viewing area.
9. Walking distance to Hooters.
8. Radio play-by-play broadcast by loudspeakers under the stands (especially when Jon Miller was there).
7. Field-level out-of-town scoreboard.
6. All seats are a rich, soothing dark green.
5. Seven-foot outfield wall allows for highlight-reel catches.
4. The E in THE SUN sign on the scoreboard lights up when there's an error, and the H lights up when a questionable play is officially ruled a hit.
3. Orioles neon-orange letters atop scoreboard clock, flanked by Oriole-bird weather vanes.
2. Eutaw Street Pavilion. The most unique walkway of any stadium in the country. And the best thing about Camden Yards
1. The Warehouse.

THE WAREHOUSE: Oriole Park at Camden Yards' most distinct feature is the B&O Railroad Warehouse, the longest building on the East coast at 1,016 feet (but only 51 feet wide). The brick structure, built between 1898-1905, is 432 feet from home plate and now houses the Orioles' offices, a baseball store, cafeteria (Pastimes) and a bar/lounge (Bambino's).

Inside, the Orioles have preserved the original brick, leaving its walls exposed. Inside are arguably the best office-window views in the country (a view of the ballpark, of course). A glass-encased model of Camden Yards greets visitors on the second floor as they step off the elevator, and an enlarged, panoramic photo of the last major league baseball game played at Memorial Stadium graces the wall in front of the Orioles' receptionist.

So far those windows have been in little danger of being shattered, but it's bound to happen some day. It took a year and a half before a ball reached the building.

THIS YEAR, A PARTICULARLY CARNIVAL-LIKE ATMOSPHERE AT THE ALL-STAR GAME...

JUNIOR'S ACHIEVEMENT: *Baseball Weekly* senior writer Tim Wendel was one week out of a sling from a softball collarbone injury and covering the 1993 All-Star festivities at Camden Yards. He and former Orioles public relations director Rick Vaughn had chosen a vantage point along the Eutaw Street Pavilion. Wendel was sitting on a café-style table and leaning against the warehouse. "(Dave) Justice was batting and just pulled this one pitch," Wendel said. "The ball was coming right at me. At first I thought it was going to hit the warehouse but it landed in front of me. It bounced off the sidewalk into the air and then hit the wall. About 100 fans started running right toward me. I ducked under the table as everybody went over me for that ball. If I hadn't, I would've re-broken my collarbone and probably have broken the other one. I would've ended up looking like some kind of cartoon character."

Once the commotion had stopped, Wendel emerged intact and was there to document history. The next batter was Ken Griffey Jr., the first man ever to hit the warehouse with a batted ball.

JEWEL OF THE CITY: The success of Oriole Park triggered a slew of copy cats. Suddenly every team with a cookie-cutter, multipurpose stadium built in the last 30 years wanted a baseball-only showcase, too.

"Camden Yards is more successful than Baltimore city officials ever imagined, boosting community pride, economic prosperity and something resembling spirituality about the game," wrote Karen Hucks of the *Tacoma News-Tribune*. "It's now widely perceived as Baltimore's single greatest source of community pride.

"Sidewalks are mobbed with vendors, diners, pub crawlers and sightseers. New restaurants have cropped up and at least one hotel has doubled in size.

"Oriole Park has changed the face of the city, its neighborhoods and its business community … During the first season in 1992, the park brought 1.6 million out-of-town fans – 46% of the attendees – to metropolitan Baltimore, a city survey of fans concluded. That was 76% more tourism than during Memorial Stadium years.

"Fans in 1992 spent $38.1 million in the downtown area, outside the ballpark, and $15 million in suburban areas. And in subsequent years, attendance didn't level off, as is usually expected."

The O's lure a well-dressed crowd.

YOU CAN'T YANK THE O'S AROUND: Sure, everyone wants admission to Camden Yards – particularly FREE admission. "It's a constant battle to keep the 'Foofs' out," said Orioles assistant PR director Bill Stetka. (For those who don't know, and that's almost everybody, a "Foof" is a fan posing as a member of the media.) "One time we received a handwritten request for seven credentials from a New York publication. But it was just for one game of a Yankees series, which was unusual; if you're covering the team you'd want them for the whole series.

"I called the Yankees' PR director and he had never heard of the publication. So I called the fellow who had made the request, and it turns out it was a community association newsletter. Seven of the members were taking a trip to Baltimore and wanted to write about what it was like going to a game at Camden Yards."

Stetka suggested it might work out a little better if they purchased tickets instead.

NO GO FOR KATO: One of the most famous "Foofs" to try to finagle free tickets was Kato Kaelin, who experienced his "fifteen minutes of fame" as a witness in the O.J. Simpson trial. In 1995 he asked the Orioles if he could throw out the ceremonial first pitch at a game. The team said no. Then he requested a press credential so he could schmooze on the field with players before the game. The team said no again.

ILLUSTRATING A POINT: Those Yankees fans. Nobody is less welcome in Camden Yards than they. Check out this classic from the Oct. 27, 1997 issue of *Sports Illustrated*:

"In their series' five years on NBC, the producers of "Homicide: Life on the Street" have used police tape to cordon off fictitious murder scenes on streets and back alleys all over Baltimore. But the show had never tried to stage a crime at the city's best-known setting: Oriole Park at Camden Yards. The idea that Peter Angelos, the owner of the Baltimore Orioles, and the Maryland Stadium Authority would permit "Homicide" to portray some grisly murder there, made-for-TV or not, seemed hopelessly far-fetched.

"But in what producers David Simon and Jim Yoshimura describe as a moment of 'pure, unencumbered genius,' they jiggered the plot so that the ballpark brass not only embraced the idea but also happily allowed Orioles pitchers Armando Benitez and Scott Erickson to make cameo appearances. In this season's second episode, the victim and the killer are both obnoxious men with thick Long Island accents. Each is a New York Yankees fan. 'Someone should check the Maryland Annotated Code,' says Detective John Munch, who is played by Richard Belzer. 'I'm not sure this is actually a crime in Baltimore.' "

	1	2	3	4	5	6	7	8	9	F
Visitor	0	0	0							
Orioles	1	1	1							

THIRD INNING

Never a dull moment

"Tweedle-dee-dee, tweedle-dee-dum. Look out, baby, now here I come." – Rare Earth, "Get Ready," 1970.

A steady stream of celebrities have made their way to Baltimore for baseball. The Orioles have had three visits by President Bill Clinton ('93, '95 and '96). When he arrives, he's always accompanied not only by hordes of security but also by the White House Press. "We have to remind them that there is a game going on," O's assistant public relations director Bill Stetka said, "and the president isn't the main event."

Clinton and Vice President Al Gore became the first President and Vice President in history to attend a sporting event together outside Washington, DC. They were both there for Cal Ripken's 2,131st consecutive game Sept. 6, 1995.

In May of 1991 Queen Elizabeth accompanied President George Bush to a game, and in 1989 Bush hosted the president of Egypt, Hosni Mubarak. Sandra Day O'Connor recently had her picture taken in an Orioles uniform with Cal Ripken. Season-ticket holders include Tim Russert of "Meet The Press" and *Washington Post* columnist George Will.

Since moving to Camden Yards, the Orioles have been popular with athletes from other sports. Golfers Scott Simpson – who is buddies with Jesse Orosco – and Ben Crenshaw have been to games. NBA stars Reggie Miller, Joe Smith and Mark Jackson love coming to games. Any NBA player who visits town usually wants to meet Cal Ripken, and he generally wants to meet them. An avid hoopster, Ripken has his own indoor, full-court gym and recruits them for his home pickup games.

Rock-and-roller Joan Jett is a big Orioles fan. She has sung the national anthem in Baltimore several times, and one year even attended an Orioles Fantasy Camp. Other musical artists to have been Orioles guests include Jewel and Hootie and the Blowfish.

Hollywood actors Kevin Costner, Corbin Bernsen, John Lithgow and others have visited Camden Yards.

'DAVE' GETS SAVED: Speaking of Hollywood, several movies have used Camden Yards for scenes, including "Major League 2" and "Dave."

In a scene from "Dave," a presidential look-alike, Kevin Kline, is asked to fill in for the President himself. Of course one of the President's duties is to throw out the first pitch on Opening Day. In the film they decided to do this in front of an actual Camden Yards crowd. Before the game, Rex Barney, the Orioles' late public address announcer, proclaimed, "Ladies and Gentlemen, the President of the United States!" Kline walked out and threw a pitch to Orioles catcher Jeff Tackett. According to Orioles assistant PR director Bill Stetka, "Kline is not an athletic man. He tried three pitches and never came close to Tackett." Fans were cracking up in the stands, laughing hysterically. "Finally, they decided to use then-Orioles PR director Rick Vaughn, who had pitched in high school," Stetka said. They shot him from behind. He put the pitch right in there."

GATE ATTRACTIONS: Kline should be embarrassed, particularly since a mother of quintuplets, Pamela Pisner, successfully threw out the first pitch at Camden Yards on Mother's Day, 1997.

It was part of a unique Mother's Day at the ballpark. Players stood at each gate and handed out long-stemmed carnations to all the arriving women.

"I didn't expect this," Diane Koblinsky of Glen Burnie, Md. told *Baseball Weekly*. "I was pleased and surprised."

Although there were several players at each gate, the hot spot was Gate A, manned by Cal Ripken and Brady Anderson.

"We were going to come in another gate, but we saw the crowd here and came over to see what everyone was looking at," said Michelle Cashour of Linthicum, Md. She arrived with her mother, Pat, and son, Justin. "Cal gave flowers to my mom and me and a high-five to Justin."

The players handed out between 10,000 and 20,000 carnations on that day.

NET GAINS: Celebrities don't just frequent Orioles games. Some of them actually own a piece of the team. Among the club's investors are movie producer/director/writer Barry Levinson, ABC-TV sports commentator Jim McKay and professional tennis player Pam Shriver. Novelist Tom Clancy is the club's vice chairman of community projects and public affairs, but he keeps a low profile.

The same can't be said for Shriver, who invited Orioles Roberto Alomar and Brady Anderson to play in a 1997 charity tennis event held at the Baltimore Arena.

Instead of Cal Ripken or Mike Bordick, Alomar's double play partner – or should we say "doubles" play partner – was Monica Seles.

Anderson and Mary Joe Fernandez beat Alomar and Seles 4-2 in the one-set exhibition. Then everybody switched sides and the two Birds played the two women's tennis stars to a 1-1 standoff in two games.

The funniest part of the event occurred when a hard shot by Fernandez whizzed past Anderson's head.

"Hey, take it easy," said Shriver, handling public-address commentary for the match. "We just exercised a $4 million option on this guy. He's our star."

SPITGATE: The tennis tournament was a good time for Alomar, who is best-remembered for something not so jovial. If Gaylord Perry is known for throwing the spitter, Alomar is known for being thrown out for spitting.

Actually, Alomar was thrown out of the game before his famous expectoration. It was Friday, Sept. 27, 1996, in the first inning of a game against Toronto. Plate umpire John Hirschbeck had just called Alomar out on strikes on a pitch several inches outside the strike zone. After the obligatory back-and-forth, Hirschbeck followed Alomar to the dugout and ejected him. Alomar, just a tad upset, bolted from the dugout and went face-to-face with Hirschbeck.

Alomar took personal offense to a Hirschbeck insult and spit in the umpire's face, drawing what many observers believed to be a not-serious-enough five-game suspension.

Of course, newspaper copy editors, many of whom love bad puns, had a field day with headline possibilities: Spit Happens, Same Old Spit, Great Expectorations, Alomar's in Hock Now, Robbed of Dignity, Spit Hits The Fans and Ban The Spitter.

HE'S A YANKEE FAN, YADA YADA: Jerry Seinfeld, star of the immensely-popular TV show "Seinfeld," was in Baltimore for a comedy benefit and tried to squeeze in a game. He arrived at the ballpark in the seventh inning and went to his seat in the fifth row behind home plate. He had security all around him but people spotted him and before long the fans began chanting "Jer-ry! Jer-ry! Jer-ry!" This went on for two innings. In the ninth inning the Orioles put Seinfeld's picture on the scoreboard and introduced him. He reached under his seat and put on an Orioles cap. This was no small stunt, since he's a well-known Yankees fan (not that there's anything wrong with that). Even so, the fans gave Seinfeld a standing ovation.

THANK GOD I'M AN ORIOLES FAN: For almost 20 years, the late John Denver's 1975 hit "Thank God I'm A Country Boy" has been played over the PA system during the seventh-inning stretch at Orioles games. Even fans in Camden Yards' corporate boxes

John Denver: God bless 'im.

whoop and clap the words. The song first caught on in 1979, a World Series season for the O's. It was a fun, upbeat song that got people clapping. "They played it a while. When they stopped, people booed," Orioles assistant PR director Bill Stetka said. "So they started playing it every night."

Denver performed the song atop the dugout during the 1983 World Series, and in 1991 agreed informally to perform the song again if Baltimore ever returned to the Fall Classic. Sadly, that will never happen. Denver, 53, died in a plane crash in October 1997. Only a few months earlier, Denver had danced and clapped along to the song atop the Orioles dugout as a guest of the Orioles.

YOU JUST MISSED HIM: Another instance of top-of-the-dugout-dancing wasn't quite so popular, at least with one fellow. During the first year of interleague play, 1997, the Orioles had swept the Phillies in a three-game series, and near the end of the third game the Oriole Bird was dancing atop the Philadelphia dugout with a broom. Phillies third base coach John Vukovich viewed the Bird's antics with more than mild displeasure. After the game he marched to the mascot dressing room. The man playing the Bird, Bromley Lowe, had already doffed his costume and changed into street clothes when Vukovich rapped on the door.

"Where's that mascot?" Vukovich said angrily.

"Oh, he just left," Lowe said. "But I'll be sure to tell him you came by."

ALTOBELLI WENT BELLY-UP: Then-Orioles owner Edward Bennett Williams didn't think much of manager Joe Altobelli, even though he led the team to the 1983 World Championship. "If anybody had managed that team, we would have won," Williams said.

According to author Peter Richmond's *Ballpark*, Altobelli responded, "He also called me 'cement head,' but that doesn't make him right."

Someone asked Williams if, indeed, he had called his manager "cement head." The owner wasn't sure, but, he said, "it wasn't inconsistent with my thinking on the subject."

On Aug. 24, 1984, Altobelli had managed himself into a situation against Toronto where infielder Lenn Sakata was playing catcher and outfielders Gary Roenicke and John Lowenstein were playing third and second base, respectively.

"Tippy Martinez came in with none out and a man at first," freelance writer Louis Berney said. "He picked that man off. A second man got on base, and he picked him off, too. It was a tight game, you see, and the Blue Jays figured they could steal on Sakata. A third man got on base, and Tippy picked him off, too. He picked off three guys in one inning. It was one of the most incredible feats in Orioles history."

Martinez saved Altobelli that day, but Williams remained convinced Earl Weaver would never have been in that situation in the first place.

	1	2	3	4	5	6	7	8	9	F
Visitor	0	0	0	0						
Orioles	1	1	1	1						

FOURTH INNING

Earl

"It's what you learn after you know it all that counts." – Earl Weaver, 1968.

In the lexicon of sports, some personalities are so big a single name suffices. Magic. Bird. Junior. Michael.

In Baltimore, there is Earl.

Earl Weaver was a Rare Bird indeed: A manager who stayed in the business for 17 seasons with one team and was never fired. In fact, the Orioles hired him TWICE. How many men can make such a claim?

Although diminutive, Weaver defined the term "feisty." During an animated argument, he loved to kick dirt and swing his cap around backward to get his 5-foot-7 frame under an umpire's chin. A recent article in *The Washington Post* defined Weaver as "a piece of work."

"I got thrown out, what was it, 91 times?" Weaver asked *Baseball Weekly's* Bill Koenig. "Think about how many calls the umpires made, all the balls and strikes. Millions of calls. And the umps only got 91 of them wrong."

MOUND OF EXPERIENCE: Yes, Weaver was ejected 91 times, two of them coming in both ends of a doubleheader. "Earl's bark was worse than his bite, but you had to know him and kind of grow up with him, and then you loved him like a father," former

Orioles manager Davey Johnson told Koenig. "He was a used-car salesman in the minor leagues during the offseason, so he learned a lot of ways to sell you on just about anything."

Weaver was the kind of guy who loved an angle, a way to get any kind of advantage he could.

"Did you ever notice that Earl always goes to the highest spot on the mound when he comes out?" O's pitching great Jim Palmer once said.

But Palmer benefited from Weaver's angles, too. Before the trees behind the outfield wall at Memorial Stadium grew up, Earl Weaver would start Palmer on every Sunday at home so that his overhand fastball would come straight out of the white facades of the homes on 37th Street.

WEAVER'S WINNING WAYS: It's easy to understand why Weaver was never fired: He won, and won big, compiling a 1480-1060 record. His .583 winning percentage ranks seventh among managers this century. He won 100-plus games five times, including 109 in '69 and 108 in '70. He collected six AL East titles and four pennants after he took over the Orioles on July 11, 1968. Weaver led Baltimore to the World Series in his first full season, although his team was upset by the Miracle Mets of 1969. A year later, the Orioles rebounded with a five-game Series win against Cincinnati.

Weaver prided himself on his baseball judgment. He knew how 25 players fit on a team. He told Koenig that his judgment said Boog Powell, Dave McNally and Andy Etchebarren could be major leaguers when not everyone in the organization was convinced. "Davey Johnson was the only player everybody was sure about," Weaver said.

A GREAT ONE: According to baseball scholar Bill James, Weaver was one of the 10 most successful managers of all time. He won 420 more games than he lost, ranking him sixth on the alltime list in that category (there are only 36 managers in baseball history who finished their careers 100 games over .500). Using an intricate formula that we won't get into here, James ranked Weaver the No. 7 manager ever, tied with Harry Wright. Only John McGraw, Connie Mack, Joe McCarthy, Casey Stengel, Walter Alston and Sparky Anderson were ranked higher than Weaver.

WHAT KIND OF MANAGER WAS WEAVER? He was intense. A decision-maker. He loved to platoon. He used everybody on his roster. He favored veteran role players. He hated to bunt (by the end of his career he was down to about 30 bunts a season). He wasn't much for the running game. He rarely used the hit-and-run. He favored veteran pitchers who threw strikes. He used a four-man rotation, pitched them deep into the game, and somehow kept them healthy. He was the most outspoken advocate of the big inning in baseball history.

EARL'S NOSEPRINTS ON 106 UMPIRES' NOSES...

Perhaps his greatest asset was that he knew a team's limitations. He was to managers what Larry Bird was to NBA superstars.

According to Bill James, "what he liked to do was take two or three veteran minor leaguers, each of whom was one or two tools short of a whole package, and try to find some way to use them that would hide their weaknesses and make maximum use of what they did well. He had great success with guys like Pat Kelly, Larry Harlow, Andres Mora, Terry Crowley, John Lowenstein and Benny Ayala, who for the most part would never have gotten more than a cup of coffee with other teams."

He also recognized talent, nurturing and turning the likes of Bobby Grich, Doug DeCinces, Don Baylor, Eddie Murray, Cal Ripken, Al Bumbry, Rich Dauer, Rick Dempsey, Elrod Hendricks and Merv Rettenmund into starters.

That was important, because from 1975-78 the Orioles were losing many big-name free agents. Nevertheless, he kept the team winning around 90 games a season. "This is the most impressive part of his record," James wrote in 1997.

At least one fan laments those bygone days. "The Orioles used to be the anti-Yankees," said John Hunt, who writes a national fantasy baseball column for *Baseball Weekly*. "They used to get guys nobody else wanted and make them winners. The whole was so much greater than the sum of their parts. Guys like Joe Orsulak and Jim Dwyer couldn't play on any other team, but they were great Orioles. Gary Roenicke was a total washout everywhere else, but a great Oriole. These days, the team just goes for the high-priced stars.

"The Orioles have become the Yankees."

MAXIMIZING HIS ASSETS: Weaver would not have a player on his roster who wasn't exceptional in some fashion. He could be a light-hitting infielder as long as he was exceptional in the field. He could be slow and have no arm as long as he could knock in a key run as a pinch-hitter. "What Weaver NEVER used were the guys who didn't do anything specific, the .260 hitters with 10 to 15 homers, a little speed and so-so defense," James wrote.

He had carefully defined roles for every player on his roster and he used them all. "If he had 30 men, he would have started pinch-hitting in the fourth inning," wrote James.

He would put three or four defensive specialists in his starting lineup then pinch-hit for them with outfielders who were considered rejects by other teams. All managers do this, but Weaver did it more than anybody ever.

HE WAS A REAL CARD: According to Peter Richmond's *Ballpark*, Weaver had a special pocket sewn into the inside of the lapel of his baseball jersey to carry cigarettes. He used to like to stand naked in his office after games, bare feet on a cement floor, a cigarette in one hand, a can of National Bohemian beer (with salt) in the other, the radiator hissing in the corner.

No doubt he'd be playing the game back in his mind. He was known for keeping detailed index cards on each opponent.

"He was far ahead of his time," new Orioles manager Ray Miller told *Baseball Weekly's* Bill Koenig. "He did it long before everybody had computers. He was absolutely the best at getting the right guy up to bat at the right time."

The cards didn't just help Weaver win games. It also helped him deal with the media.

"Weaver was very media-savvy," Orioles assistant PR director Bill Stetka said. "After the game he'd go to his office and pore over his index cards, thinking about what he was going to say. He'd try to anticipate what the reporters were going to ask and head them off. He held court well, but he was a tough little guy to be around.

"When I was a young sportswriter, he'd tell me, 'You'll go a long way if you listen to me.' That was his way of keeping you from asking the tough questions."

A SPIRITED EXCHANGE: Weaver once was upset with Pat Kelly, a Christian. Kelly responded by telling Weaver, "Walk with the Lord." Weaver replied, "I'd rather you walk with the bases loaded."

NOW THE MARRIOTT, THAT'S DIFFERENT ...: After retiring at the end of the 1982 season, Weaver returned to manage the Orioles in mid-1985.

"Economics played a role," Weaver told *The Sporting News* of his decision to return. "Raleighs have gone from $6.50 to $9 a carton, but there's a 3/4-cent coupon on the back. You can get all kinds of things with them – blenders, everything. I saved up enough one time and got Al Bumbry."

Weaver retired for good in 1986, citing travel demands as a primary factor in his decision. "What scares the hell out of me is waking up dead some morning in the Hyatt Hotel in Oakland," he said.

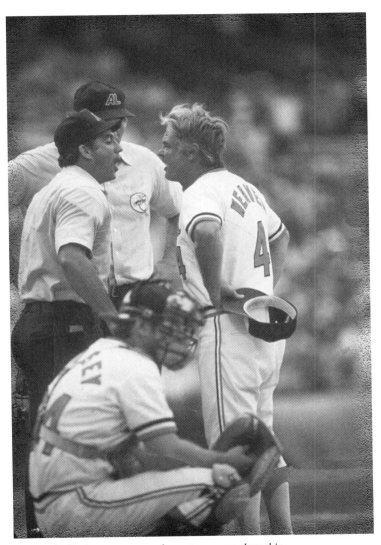

Just wait: Earl can get even closer to an ump than this.

THE NEWS WASN'T BOGUS; IT WAS BOGEY-US: Today Weaver resides in the Miami area. His typical day includes getting on the golf course by 11:30 a.m. Before he knows it, it's 3:30. "One of the reasons I retired," Weaver told *Baseball Weekly's* Bill Koenig, "was so I could have dinner at home and a cocktail or two before."

Time flies on the course for Weaver because he's completely immersed in the game. He's still a competitor.

"Earl didn't give you a chance on the golf course," former Oriole Davey Johnson told Koenig. "He made you give him enough strokes so that if he played bad, he'd still beat you. I managed to tie him a few times, and that's about it." And Johnson is nearly a scratch golfer.

Fittingly, Weaver was about 90 yards from the pin at the ninth hole of a Miami area golf course when his wife, Marianna, arrived on a golf cart to deliver the news that Weaver had been voted into the Hall of Fame.

"My knees got weak and my body got weak," he said. "I ended up bogeying the hole."

(FUTURE) MEMBERSHIP HAS ITS PRIVILEGES: The Hall of Fame Veterans Committee inducted Weaver August 4, 1996, an event that was generally considered a formality – and not just in Baltimore. Earlier that year, in Fort Myers, Fla., Weaver strided into a reception reserved for those already enshrined. "The guy at the door thought I was already in the Hall of Fame," Weaver told Koenig. "He let me right in. Well, I got some free beer."

AND A DARN GOOD ONE, TOO: Weaver's life was baseball. Without it, according to Bill James, Weaver would have been "a bouncer at a midget bar."

ENOUGH SAID: Although Weaver was as well-known for his fights with his players, he didn't need to spend a lot of time talking to his stars.

"Frank (Robinson) and I, in the course of the season, didn't have more than 30 conversations," Weaver told Koenig. That wasn't the case with Weaver and star pitcher Jim Palmer, however.

AN ODD COUPLE: Palmer and Weaver. The names forever interwoven. Both brilliant, they bickered but both knew where their bread was buttered and, when it came right down to it, respected each other immensely...we think. Palmer once said, "I don't want to win my 300th game while Earl is still here. He'd take credit for it."

Countered Weaver back in the 1970s: "I have more fights with Jim Palmer than my wife. The Chinese tell time by the 'Year of the Horse' or the 'Year of the Dragon.' I tell time by the 'Year of the Back' or the 'Year of the Elbow.' Every time Palmer reads about a new ailment, he seems to get it. This year it's the 'Year of the Ulnar Nerve.' Someone once asked me if I had any physical incapacities of my own. Know what I answered? 'Sure I do. One big one: Jim Palmer.' "

During a Ft. Lauderdale press conference to promote his new book, *Together We Were Eleven Foot Nine*, Palmer found a way to have the last word with Weaver.

Palmer was there in person, but Weaver instead was represented by a life-sized cutout complete with Baltimore uniform . . . and a sock tied around its mouth.

"This is the Earl many umpires wish they could've had," Palmer told Pete Williams of *Baseball Weekly*.

Palmer said the book is about his 20-year love/hate relationship with Weaver. "I thought it was the perfect idea for a book," Palmer told Williams. "Especially when Earl said he wasn't going to read it. "So what do you think of the book, Earl?" Palmer said. "Oh, you love it? Good, good."

	1	2	3	4	5	6	7	8	9	F
Visitor	0	0	0	0	0					
Orioles	1	1	1	1	1					

FIFTH INNING

The Pitchers

"If you know how to cheat, start now." – Earl Weaver, on the mound, to struggling Russ Grimsley.

When you think of 20-game winners, you think of the Baltimore Orioles. Although they haven't had one in the last 14 years, the club has still produced twenty-four 20-game winners since 1968, prohibitively more than any other major league club. The Oakland Athletics are next with 14, followed by the New York Yankees and Chicago White Sox (11 each) and Los Angeles Dodgers (10). And in this era of five-man rotations, don't expect the gap to be closed any time soon.

From 1968 through 1980, a span of 13 years, at least one Oriole pitcher accumulated 20 or more victories, setting a major league record.

In 1971, four Baltimore pitchers reached the 20-win plateau. That has happened only one other time in major league history, by the 1920 White Sox.

Dave McNally – who once won 17 consecutive games, and 13 another time – was the first O's pitcher to collect his 20th win that season, on Sept. 21. The other three did it in one series against Cleveland. Mike Cuellar won the first game of a doubleheader on Sept. 24, a victory that clinched a division title. Then, in the second game of the doubleheader, Pat Dobson notched his 20th.

Jim Palmer picked up his 20th win on Sept. 26.

Even the great '90s Atlanta Braves staffs of Greg Maddux, John Smoltz, Tom Glavine and Steve Avery/Denny Neagle never came close to achieving what the Orioles staff did in 1971.

THANKS FOR THE REMINDER: Pitching isn't all business. A little humor can go a long way in loosening a guy up, and Johnny Oates, then a catcher for the Orioles who later became manager for the club, knew this. Reliever Doyle Alexander was pitching for the first time in a couple of weeks, coming back from a minor injury. "When I got to the mound," Alexander said, "Johnny reminded me that the lower mask was his and the upper one was the umpire's."

SCOTT MCGREGOR: Left-hander Scott McGregor's prime was 1978-85. In that eight-year stretch he was the only pitcher in baseball with a record over .500 in each of those seasons. In 1983 he won 16 of his last 17 decisions on the road. He pitched the World Series clincher in 1983. His secret: three pitches thrown at three distinctly different speeds yet by the same odd, across-the-body motion. He threw an 86-mph fastball, 73-mph changeup and 63-mph curve.

In Game One of the 1983 World Series, after the Orioles hit in the seventh, McGregor was all set to pitch when a crewman for ABC waved him off. "There is a certain flow to the game," McGregor told *Sports Illustrated*. "I told that guy never to do that to me again. He already had five minutes. I said, 'Sell your Datsuns some other way.' (That would be Nissans today.)

In reality, ABC was holding up the game because announcer Howard Cosell was in the stands interviewing President Ronald Reagan. The President, for the record, was wearing a bright red turtleneck under a tweed sports coat.

Today McGregor serves as pastor for the Rock Church in Dover, Del. He retired when his fastball dropped into the 70s. "My last two years were just horrible," he told *Baseball Weekly's* Scott Zucker. "My name was like a standing boo-vation."

It was easy to rally behind Dave McNally.

IT WASN'T MUSIC TO MYERS' EARS: McGregor wasn't the only Orioles pitcher to get irked with off-field shenanigans. According to *Baseball Weekly*, reliever Randy Myers found a new outlet for a 1997 3-2 loss to Seattle: the sound man in the control room at Camden Yards.

With Seattle's Alex Rodriguez at the plate in the 10th inning, Myers was in the middle of his windup when several notes of a song inadvertently blared over the P.A. system. Myers stopped abruptly and said later he pulled a muscle in the process.

He lost the game on Mike Blowers' pinch-hit single in the 11th inning.

"That screwed me up the rest of the day," Myers said. "They ought to just fire the guy. Everyone knows you can't play music during at-bats."

Nobody was fired.

A GAME TO FORGET: Maybe somebody should have gotten fired on June 19, 1991. The Orioles were playing Minnesota in Baltimore. Twins outfielder Shane Mack came to the plate in the ninth inning with the bases loaded and the score tied 4-4. He swung – and missed – at only one pitch, but before his at-bat ended in a walk, the bases were empty and Minnesota had scored three runs. The runners came home on three wild pitches and a throwing error by Oriole reliever Gregg Olson.

GREGG OR GREG? GEE, THEY DON'T KNOW: If that wasn't bad enough for Olson, then consider his problem with the U.S. Postal Service. In the early 1990s his mail kept getting sent to Atlanta Braves catcher Greg Olson. "How in the world can someone write a letter to an Orioles' pitcher and send it to Atlanta?" Greg asked *Sports Illustrated* in 1990. "I must have 50 letters of his. This winter was ridiculous. I got 18 fan letters at my home, and 17 were for him. With the first few I wrote back and said, 'You have the wrong Gregg Olson.' After that, I kept 'em. I have more Greg Olson baseball cards [enclosed in the letters in hope that Olson would autograph and return them] than anyone in America."

Scott McGregor: A master of keeping hitters off-balance.

SO WHO WAS CY OF RELIEF? Left-hander Mike Flanagan won the 1979 Cy Young Award, going 23-9. According to Ted Patterson's coffee table book *The Baltimore Orioles*, Flanagan was doing Chris Berman nicknames before Berman made the game popular on ESPN's "SportsCenter."

Twins infielder John Castino was "Clams," while Ruben Sierra became Ruben Scare-ya.

In 1980 Flanagan dubbed himself Cy Young, since he was the

most-recent recipient, and Jim Palmer, who had won it in 1973, '75 and '76, was Cy Old. Steve Stone won it in 1980, so he was Cy Present. Promising young Scott McGregor was Cy Future and Storm Davis, a Palmer pitch-alike, was Cy Clone. Any injured pitcher was Cy Bex and a pitcher on his way out was Cy-Anarah.

ONE FUNNY GUY: "I could never play in New York," Flanagan said. "The first time I ever came into a game there, I got into the bullpen cart and they told me to lock the door."

After fellow pitcher Mike Boddicker's fastball was clocked at 88 mph against Toronto, Flanagan said, "We forgot about the Canadian exchange rate, so it's really only 82 mph."

JIM PALMER – PITCHING AND PANCAKES: As great as all the Orioles pitchers were, the only one to have had his number retired by the ball club was Jim Palmer.

Former O's outfielder Merv Rettenmund (1968-73) was once asked if he'd rather face Jim Palmer or Tom Seaver. "That's like asking whether I'd rather be hung or go to the electric chair," he said.

Palmer was offered a basketball scholarship to UCLA by the great John Wooden. He collected eight 20-win seasons, 12 with at least 15 wins and won three Cy Young awards. He had a 2.85 ERA, ranking him fourth all-time behind Walter Johnson, Grover Cleveland Alexander and Whitey Ford.

When Palmer was just 21 years old, he won seven of eight starts after eating pancakes for breakfast. Pancakes became standard fare for him on the days he pitched, and he earned the nickname "Cakes."

An easy Hall-of-Fame choice, Palmer never set out for greatness. "I read where Roger Clemens said making the Hall of Fame was a goal of his," Palmer said at the time of his election in early 1990. "To me, that's like planning for the ninth inning when you're in first. I don't know many players who've set out to make the Hall of Fame, and I played with both Frank and Brooks Robinson. I remember talking to Brooks about it one time, and it was like it had not even occurred to him. If Brooks Robinson didn't have the right to think about it, who did?"

THE MOOSE IS LOOSE: The mantle of past pitching greatness has now been passed on to right-hander Mike Mussina, a man who has openly admitted, "I couldn't see myself playing in another uniform."

Rather than test the more lucrative waters of free agency after the 1997 season, the Orioles' ace, 28 at the time, agreed to a three-year, $21.5 million contract.

"I think sometimes you don't know what you have until you don't have it anymore," Mussina told *Baseball Weekly*. In 1997, "Moose" had the highest winning percentage of any active pitcher with 50 or more decisions. "I love coming to the ballpark," he said. To come to the ballpark here every day, to have the place filled to the top 90% of the time – we have great fans. . . . It's just fun to play baseball here."

Left Photo: Jim Palmer: A short "weight" for Hall of Fame induction.

	1	2	3	4	5	6	7	8	9	F
Visitor	0	0	0	0	0	0				
Orioles	1	1	1	1	1	1				

SIXTH INNING
Cal and The Streak

"Cal Ripken is no different from anyone else, except that he's doing something no one else has ever done or ever will do."
– Davey Johnson, former Orioles Manager

When Cal Ripken started his streak on Sunday, May 30, 1982, nobody had heard about El Niño, there was no such thing as Microsoft, Steven Spielberg's "E.T." was being shown as a sneak preview along with Steve Martin's "Dead Men Don't Wear Plaid," people were using typewriters instead of PCs, the Go-Gos were a hot new band and NBA basketball shorts were actually short.

Nobody knew they were going to be part of history that day. Ripken, a 21-year-old rookie, batted eighth, played third base and went 0-for-2 with a strikeout, walk and groundout to shortstop in a 6-0 loss to the Toronto Blue Jays.

In a 1995 *Sporting News* article by Dennis Tuttle, pitcher Jim Gott remembered the beginning of The Streak. "He was a contemporary of mine, a young guy we'd heard a lot about," Gott told Tuttle. "In the pitchers and catchers meeting before the game, I was in Bobby Cox's office with Al Widmar, Buck Martinez and Ernie Whitt going over the hitters.

"When Cal's name came up, everybody got a puzzled look ... (but) everybody said to be careful because the reports were that he was a good low-ball hitter."

Hats off to Cal!

Earl Weaver had put Ripken in the lineup that day, and nobody has dared take him out since. He broke Lou Gehrig's record on Sept. 6, 1995, by playing in his 2,131st consecutive game. No Oriole fan will forget that night, when Cal took his triumphant lap around Camden Yards, slapping hands with the fans in the stands. It will go down as one of the great images in baseball history. What's amazing, though, is that since he broke that mark, he's kept going.

Is it simply coincidence that Ripken's number, sideways, looks like an infinity sign? His games played streak goes on, and on, and on …

Consider that SINCE the day Ripken broke Gehrig's mark, through the end of the 1997 season, only two other major leaguers – Houston's Craig Biggio and Jeff Bagwell – had played in all of their team's games. It's ridiculous when you think about it, really.

THAT WAS A CLOSE ONE: Cal Ripken almost stole the show during the 1996 All-Star Game when he suffered a broken nose during, of all things, the pregame team photo.

While dismounting a three-tiered platform in center field, Ripken caught a forearm from then-Chicago White Sox reliever Roberto Hernandez.

Doctors reset Ripken's nose and cleared him to start his 13th consecutive All-Star Game.

"I didn't want it to go down in the history of the All-Star Game as the only injury sustained during the team picture," a visibly embarrassed Ripken told *Baseball Weekly*.

"I was praying he'd come out there," Hernandez said. "Once he did, I said, 'All right, his streak is still alive.' "

Wow. 2,131. Seems like a lot of games ago.

Ripken had a couple of other close calls, where his streak nearly came to an end. The closest he's ever come to missing a game, he said, came after he twisted his right knee June 6, 1993 after his spikes caught in the infield grass during an O's-Mariners melee. He didn't come out of the game, but the knee was swollen and painful the next day. Even so, he didn't even miss infield practice.

He said later, "It was the closest I've come to not playing."

FOXY ADS: Ripken's streak has gone beyond the awe stage to the point where you have to laugh about it. In 1996 the Fox Television Network produced a couple of humorous promotional ads playing off Ripken's achievement.

In one, according to Pete Williams of *Baseball Weekly*, Cal answered his front door and had to deal with a sarcastic mailman who claimed to have gone over 5,000 days without missing work. "I don't suppose you've had to deal with any rabid Dobermans in the field, huh, 'Mr. Streak?' " the mailman asked him.

In another one, Cal played his fictitious twin brother, Hal Ripken. The spot began with Hal sitting in his trailer home, dressed in a Hawaiian shirt and polyester pants, explaining how he and his brother duped the public.

"No one man can play that many games in a row," Hal said. With a brown bottle in one hand and a remote control in the other, Hal flipped between footage of Ripken's career. At one point, Ripken booted a ball at shortstop. "That's Cal," Hal said.

When Ripken homered at Camden Yards, Hal said, "That's me."

"Real fans," Hal/Cal said at the end, "they can tell the difference."

"It's irresponsible and shoddy journalism, but we're not going to react to it." – O's PR director John Maroon, on a newspaper's spoof reporting the end of The Streak.

THE WORLD'S IRON MAN: After breaking Gehrig's record, Ripken kept going and eventually broke Hiroshima Carp third baseman Sachio Kinugasa's world record of 2,215 consecutive games on June 14, 1996. Kinugasa, Japan's tetsu jin (Iron Man), began his streak Oct. 19, 1970 and didn't miss a game until Oct. 22, 1987. The regular season in Japan is 130 games.

USHERING IN NEW MARKS: Because of The Streak, some fans might forget that Ripken is the Orioles' all-time home run leader, and that he has hit more home runs while playing shortstop than any man in history.

Ripken broke Chicago Cub Ernie Banks' record for career home runs by a shortstop on July 15, 1993, and Camden Yards usher Roy Smith can show you the precise spot where the homer landed: Section 86, Row FF, Seat 10. Of course, that's not such a big deal, because the point at which it landed is marked with a red seat.

Ironically, it's also the spot Ripken hit May 31 with a home run that made him the Orioles' all-time total bases leader, passing Brooks Robinson. "I knew it was history, or something like that," Smith told *Baseball Weekly* when he and fellow usher Joe Krebs converged on the spot. Part of their job is to make sure nobody gets hurt when a ball flies into the stands.

Smith is a veteran of historic Ripken homers. "I was the guy," he said, "who escorted the people who caught his home runs in games 2,130 and 2,131," when Ripken tied and broke Lou Gehrig's consecutive-games record.

THEY WERE GUNNING FOR HIM EVEN THEN: Cal might not have even been alive to start The Streak if it had not been for former Orioles third baseman Doug DeCinces. In 1972, when he was just 11 years old, Cal was traveling with his father, Cal Sr., who was managing the Orioles' Class A team in Asheville, N.C. About 45 minutes before the game, a 15-year old began firing a .45-caliber pistol from the stands. DeCinces, a minor leaguer at the time, grabbed Cal and bolted for the dugout – possibly saving his life.

DeCinces, who was traded to the Angels to make room for Ripken, was a consultant to the 1992 movie "Mr. Baseball" and tutored actor Tom Selleck on how to hit.

THE HIGHEST COMPLIMENT OF ALL? Sure, Ripken is a big fan favorite. But he's also popular among his peers.

One of Ripken's 1995 game jerseys once fetched the highest price at a charity auction in San Juan, Puerto Rico: $5,200.

The bidder was outfielder Moises Alou, who had to out-bid New York Yankees star center fielder Bernie Williams and Seattle second baseman Joey Cora.

"What (Ripken) has done, I don't think anybody else is ever gonna do," Alou told *Baseball Weekly*. "I have a hard time playing 150 games. This guy played 2,000 whatever in a row.

"Besides, he signed a ball for me during the offseason after he broke (Lou Gehrig's) record for consecutive games. He said a lot of nice things to me. This is the least I can do."

YES, BUT DID HE MAKE HIS BED? According to a story by Jon Caroulis of *The Sporting News*, Ilee Short might someday put up a sign in front of her Bluefield, W.V. house telling about her most famous boarder (we'll give you one guess who it is).

Bluefield, you see, has been the home to the Orioles' rookie Appalachian League farm club for years. Many times young ballplayers would stay at her house. Instead of a college dormitory, for many it was the first time they had ever lived away from home.

In the summer of 1978, the Orioles assigned their second-round draft pick, Ripken, to Bluefield, where he stayed with Short.

"You know how some places have a sign that says, 'The President Slept Here'? Well, someday I'm going to put up a sign that says 'Cal Ripken Slept Here,' " Short, 89, told Caroulis. "He was a nice, quiet young man. Later, his father wanted me to board his brother, Billy, but I didn't have room for him."

WEAVER SEAL OF APPROVAL: Calvin Edwin Ripken Jr. has been one of the easiest men in history for managers to deal with. A skipper could automatically pencil-in Ripken for the lineup every day, and he wouldn't have to worry about much else. "Cal, you'd just tell him what to do at spring training," said Hall of Fame manager Earl Weaver, who was known for having numerous run-ins with players. "You might not have to tell him again all season."

CALL THESE IMBECILES "EMBECILES":   With all that Ripken has accomplished, you'd think people would be able to spell his name right. But *Baseball Weekly* columnist Paul White points out that isn't the case.

"Maybe names like Grudzielanek and Kamieniecki get messed up a higher percentage of the time, but on a sheer volume basis, nothing comes close to the number of RIPKINs that show up," White wrote.

"Where does the KIN come from? Is it some subconscious thing because of the Ripken kin in baseball?"

Ripken told White he was aware of the phenomenon but that it didn't bother him. Mostly, it's the executives who mess it up; kids usually get it right.

Nevertheless, it still happens more often than you'd imagine. "I see it at least a dozen times a day," said Ira Rainess, chief operating officer of the Tufton Group, the firm that handles Ripken's business affairs. "I'll open 50 pieces of correspondence (in a day) and 20% of them will have it wrong."

BOOKING CAL IS SOMETIMES EASY ...:   Ripken, of course, spells his name correctly – over and over and over again, and at all hours of the day.

During the middle of the 1997 season, Ripken conducted a book signing that didn't conclude until the wee hours of the morning.

Three-year-old Ryan Belton got his Cal Ripken autograph at 3:04 a.m., the last of about 2,200 fans who showed up that night.

After playing an extra-inning victory against the Yankees on June 3, Ripken went to a book store in suburban Towson, Md., and signed his book, *The Only Way I Know*, for 3 1/2 hours. Proceeds from the book and T-shirts sold that night went to his charity, Baltimore Reads/The Ripken Learning Center.

"I haven't stayed up this late in a long time," he told *Baseball Weekly*. "Everyone was really psyched from the game (they won

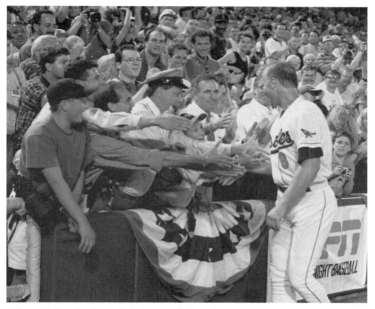

When Ripken broke Gehrig's record, Camden went crazy.

on a Rafael Palmeiro 10th-inning home run). It was easy to stay up. It was fun."

Ever-curious teammate Brady Anderson was also on hand, staying for an hour to pose for pictures.

Some of the fans waited at the store for 20 hours to be at the front of the line.

The idea came after Ripken had difficulty finding an available afternoon for the signing. He has done signings in Chicago, Seattle and New York and others in Baltimore but all in daylight hours.

... AND SOMETIMES NOT SO EASY: Cal Ripken has the reputation for being, shall we say, "exacting." While Brady Anderson sort of floats around before games, chatting with fans, hanging out in the clubhouse, stretching or whatever strikes his whim at the moment, Ripken has a strict schedule. At 3:45 p.m. he's stretching. At 3:52 he's hitting. At 5:08 he's getting taped. At 5:12 he's visiting with a kid from the Make-A-Wish Foundation.

"Before games, if someone needs Brady I can look for him and ask him if he has a minute," Orioles assistant PR director Bill Stetka said. "You can't do that with Cal. You have to plan everything in advance."

In 1994, *Baseball Weekly* senior writer Tim Wendel approached him about doing an interview. Ripken pulled out his organizer, a black, letter-sized one, and found he was free for 9 a.m. the following morning.

Wendel's habit is to show up a little early for interviews and when he went to the locker room the next day, Ripken was already there. It was 8:57 a.m.

Ripken looked at his watch. "You're early," he said.

Wendel nodded.

"Why don't you come back in about three minutes?" Ripken said.

So Wendel took a few laps around the locker room and returned three minutes later.

"It was as if Cal had rewound the clock in his head," Wendel said. "He said, 'Hey, how are you doing? Good to see you.' That's Ripken."

But he pretty much has to be that way. "Everybody wants a piece of Cal," Stetka said. "If we accommodated everybody who only wanted five minutes, he would miss a game."

And then The Streak would be over.

	1	2	3	4	5	6	7	8	9	F
Visitor	0	0	0	0	0	0	0			
Orioles	1	1	1	1	1	1	1			

SEVENTH INNING

Legends

"Brooks Robinson never asked anyone to name a candy bar after him. In Baltimore, people name their children after him." – sportswriter Gordon Beard.

Baseball icon Casey Stengel said that Brooks Robinson was the greatest third baseman he ever saw. Once, in Detroit, Robinson crashed into a concrete facade, ripping his lip and chipping five teeth, yet he stayed in the game. He was the starter in 15 consecutive All-Star games and played in 18 All-Star games overall.

"Mr. Oriole" spent 23 seasons with the club and started 20 consecutive Opening Day games. He won the AL Most Valuable Player Award in 1964. He was All-Star MVP in 1966. He was World Series MVP in 1970. He shares the record, with former pitcher Jim Kaat, for most Gold Gloves with 16. He was elected to the Hall of Fame in his first year of eligibility (1983). He was even good at setting record for dubious acts, hitting into four triple plays during his career. Who else can lay claim to that?

He was voted Orioles MVP in 1960, '62, and '64 and shared the honor with Frank Robinson in 1971. Nobody will ever wear his Orioles No. 5 again.

"Brooks was one of the most affable ballplayers ever to play for the Orioles," freelance writer Louis Berney said. "He'd talk to anybody."

Brooks Robinson: The real thing.

Robinson is probably best remembered for his fielding work in the 1970 World Series against Cincinnati, when he was dubbed "The Hoover Vacuum Cleaner" because he sucked up any ball that came his way. "He had this teeny-weeny little glove," *Baseball Weekly* columnist John Hunt said. "It was like two pancakes sewn together. He never lost a ball in that glove."

Said Brooks himself: "It's a pretty sure thing that the player's bat is what speaks loudest when it's contract time, but there are moments when the glove has the last word."

"That's his style of hitting," Yogi Berra said of Frank Robinson. *"If you can't imitate him, don't copy him."*

FRANK ROBINSON: When people talk about the greatest out-fielders of all time, they instantly think of Babe Ruth, Hank Aaron, Joe DiMaggio, Mickey Mantle, Willie Mays, Roberto Clemente, Stan Musial and Ted Williams. Knowledgeable fans mention Frank Robinson, but many casual fans won't. And that's hard to figure.

Robinson could've earned his Hall of Fame status simply for being the first black manager in major league history. Plus he was named Manager of the Year.

He was a good manager, but a great player. The man excelled in every way possible. He had great statistics, he was a winner, and he was indefatigable.

"Pitchers did me a favor when they knocked me down," he said. "It made me more determined. I wouldn't let that pitcher get me out. They say you can't hit if you're on your back. But I didn't hit on my back. I got up."

Frank Robinson: A hard man to duplicate.

If all that wasn't enough, the man even created an adage that people still use today. Everybody has heard the old saying, "close doesn't count except in horseshoes and hand grenades." According to *Baseball's Greatest Quotations* by Paul Dickson, Frank Robinson was the first to say it.

After obtaining Robinson from the Cincinnati Reds, the Orioles won four pennants and two World Series in six years. Robinson was 30 years old when he arrived in Baltimore. In 1966 he hit .316 with 49 home runs and 122 RBI and won the Triple Crown and American League MVP award. "He legitimized the Orioles," freelance writer Louis Berney said.

The Orioles went to the World Series in four of the six years he was in Baltimore. Like Brooks, Frank was elected to Cooperstown in his first year of eligibility (1982).

Robinson hit 586 career home runs and missed 3,000 hits by just 57. He would have been just the fourth man ever to reach that milestone.

He's one of only three men to have won both an MVP and a Manager of the Year award. Joe Torre and Don Baylor are the others. Baylor, an Oriole from 1970-75, won his MVP with the then-California Angels in 1979.

"Frank Robinson was tough as nails," Berney said. "He was always hard-core. But I remember at a gathering for him after the Orioles fired him as manager. He had tears in his eyes."

COURT IS IN SESSION: Robinson made his mark off the field as well. He was the man who instituted the Orioles' famous Kangaroo Court. He would place a mop on his head, don an old graduation robe and fine players who did anything silly or stupid. It was a great way to keep things loose.

BOOG POWELL: "For all of the Brooksian expertise, for all of Frank Robinson's majestic feats, no one was more of an Oriole than Boog," wrote Peter Richmond in *Ballpark*.

Powell hit 30 homers and knocked in 100 runs in 1966, 1969 and 1970. But young fans know Powell for his "Boog's Barbecue" stand at the Eutaw Street Pavilion. He was one of the

Boog Powell is 100% pure Oriole.

most exciting Orioles players ever, both on and off the field.

In the 1960s, Powell and fellow Oriole Curt Blefary would go to Colts games at Memorial Stadium. "We bought fifty-caliber ammo belts," Powell told Richmond. "See, you couldn't take (liquor) bottles into Memorial. So we bought these ammo belts at an Army-Navy surplus store and filled them with airline bottles. We'd wear them under big, loose jackets and walk right in."

Boog stood 6-4 and weighed 250 pounds and he was famous for the prodigious number of Maryland blue crabs he could put away at Bo Brooks Crab House. "If he held out his right arm, he'd be a railroad crossing," Joe Garagiola once said. Even so, he was petty nimble, especially early in his career. "People forget that he began his career as a left fielder," freelance writer Louis Berney said. "He was a very gifted fielder, tremendous with the glove."

Born John Wesley Powell, he became "Boog" as a youth because he was always getting into trouble. In the South, a kid who was always getting into trouble, knocking things over and breaking vases was called a "booger."

Today Powell is recovering from colon cancer surgery. He has drawn inspiration from Orioles outfielder Eric Davis, who had a similar operation June 13, 1997. A day after Davis had undergone one of his chemotherapy sessions, he was in the starting lineup and hit a home run and went 4-for-5 in a 5-4 win over the Milwaukee Brewers. The two have given each other moral support through chemo treatments.

EDDIE MURRAY: Between 1977 and 1988, Eddie Murray was one of the most productive Orioles ever. He hit between 25 and 35 home runs in all but one of his seasons with the Orioles, and averaged 100 RBI in each. He was named AL Rookie of the Year in 1977.

He is one of only three players in the history of major league baseball to collect 3,000 hits and 500 home runs. Hank Aaron and Willie Mays are the others. Think about it. Aaron, Mays … and Murray. Now that is some elite company.

Murray's legacy will always remain his refusal to speak with the media. He rarely had anything to say publicly and most photos showed a man with a gruff, serious face. But when an opposing batter would get to first base, he would invariably start cracking up from something Murray had said to him.

Brooks Robinson "plays the bag like he came down from a higher league."
- Umpire Ed Hurley

A LEGENDARY SQUAD: No handbook on the Orioles would be complete without an all-time team:

1B Boog Powell. With all due respect to Rafael Palmeiro.

2B Bobby Grich. With all due respect to Roberto Alomar.

3B Brooks Robinson. A no-brainer. A legend.

SS Cal Ripken. Another no-brainer. Future first-ballot Hall-of-Famer.

C Gus Triandos. Led O's in homers and RBI from 1955-58.

RF Frank Robinson. One of the greatest OFs in baseball history.

CF Brady Anderson. His 50 HRs in '96 are the most-ever by an Oriole.

LF Ken Singleton. Fifth on O's career list in hits, HR and RBIs.

DH Eddie Murray. If there was no DH, he'd have beaten out Boog.

RHP Jim Palmer. Greatest pitcher in Orioles history.

LHP Dave McNally. Second to Palmer in club wins, strike-outs, shutouts, and innings.

RP Gregg Olson.* The club's runaway career saves leader with 160.

*Randy Myers was superb in 1997. But he was only in Baltimore for two years before joining the Toronto Blue Jays. Olson was there from 1988-93.

Two more names not on that list, but deserving mention, are center fielder Paul Blair (1964-76) and shortstop Mark Belanger (1965-81).

Blair was one of the greatest defensive center fielders ever. "In the outfield, I felt there was no ball I couldn't get to," he told *Baseball Weekly's* Scott Zucker. "I played the shallowest center field of anyone. Today they don't move according to the hitter and everybody just plays deep."

Today Blair is head baseball coach at Coppin State College, teaching The Oriole Way: Don't make the little mistakes that cost you ballgames.

Belanger was one of the most beloved Orioles ever – remarkable considering he was a lifetime .228 hitter. But he won eight Gold Gloves, including six in a row. "He might not have had the range of an Ozzie Smith," said *Baseball Weekly* columnist John Hunt. "But if the ball was hit to him, the batter was out. He was as close to automatic as there's ever been at shortstop."

Belanger was so skinny, teammates called him "The Blade."

"He looked like he weighed about 120 pounds," Hunt said. "He was so skinny, his uniform would flap around him – even wearing those tight-fitting, elastic-banded polyester outfits."

He might have been thin, and quiet most of the time, but he did have his moments.

"How could he be doing his job when he didn't throw me out of the game after the things I called him?" Belanger once said after arguing with ump Russ Goetz. But umpire Ron Luciano said thumbing Belanger was easier said than done. "That's like throwing Bambi out of the forest," he said. Even so, Luciano became the first umpire ever to throw Belanger out of a game.

REX BARNEY: Although he wasn't an Orioles player, the late Rex Barney remains a true legend in Baltimore. Since the 1970s, Barney was famous for his "THANK YEEEEWWW" to fans as the O's public address announcer, and for saying "give that fan a contract!" whenever a spectator would catch a foul ball.

Originally, Barney had intoned, "Give that MAN" a contract. Then, a few games later, a long-haired fan made a good catch. "Give that WOMAN a contract," Barney said. The person turned around, and Barney realized it was a man. From then on, Barney said "fan" instead.

Barney played for the Dodgers for six seasons (1943 and 1946-50). He had a 100-mph fastball and pitched a no-hitter against the rival New York Giants at the Polo Grounds on Sept. 9, 1948. But he never was able to harness his talent. "Rex Barney would be the league's best pitcher," Bob Cooke said, "if the plate was high and outside." Nevertheless, Barney was inducted into the Brooklyn Dodgers Hall of Fame in June, 1989.

"(Barney) was one of the few PA announcers – along with the elegant Bob Sheppard at Yankee Stadium, the booming Bob

Casey in Minnesota, and the late Sherm Feller in Boston – who were part and parcel of the ballpark experience," wrote *Baseball Weekly's* Bill Koenig. "His was the reassuring 'voice' that is inexorably linked to its town."

Barney died Aug. 12, 1997 at the age of 72.

	1	2	3	4	5	6	7	8	9	F
Visitor	0	0	0	0	0	0	0	0		
Orioles	1	1	1	1	1	1	1	1		

EIGHTH INNING
The Personalities, and other fun stuff

"Enos Cabell started out with the Astros, and before that he was with the Orioles." – Announcer Jerry Coleman.

One of the greatest Orioles personalities of all time was catcher Rick Dempsey (1976-86, 1992). "The Dipper" had a .304 average in 19 postseason games. He was the 1983 World Series MVP with five hits, four doubles and a homer. He batted .385 and threw out Joe Morgan twice in three stolen base attempts.

But he was known just as well for his rain-delay antics. He came from a family of performers; his parents worked in Vaudeville and then on Broadway, so he was predisposed, to showing off. During a rain delay at Fenway Park, he stuffed pillows in his belly to resemble Baltimore native Babe Ruth. He imitated Carlton Fisk's famous 1975 home run trot. He mimicked Robin Yount in Milwaukee. In Baltimore he would slide headfirst into home plate, splashing up water all around him. And he loved to lead the O-R-I-O-L-E-S cheer from the dugout, a sort of Wild Billy Hagy in uniform.

Dempsey's legacy lives on today. He received one vote in the 1998 Hall of Fame balloting.

YEAH, BUT IT WAS THE BEST HE EVER HAD: Outfielder Jackie Brandt (1960-65) was one of the Orioles' original flakes. The team was in New York to play the Yankees and had a day off.

Rick Dempsey does Babe Ruth.

Brandt had heard about a special place that made all kinds of unique and interesting ice cream concoctions. The place had flavors you could not get anywhere else (remember, this was the early 60s). If you wanted it, they had it. There was just one catch: it was 50 miles outside of New York.

That didn't matter to Brandt, who rounded up a bunch of teammates and made the trek. When the players found the place, Brandt was first in line.

And he ordered a plain vanilla ice cream cone.

LET IT BE: Another character was John Lowenstein (1979-85). One time Lowenstein was plunked on the head with the ball and collapsed, out cold. Medics carried him off on a stretcher and the whole ballpark was deathly quiet. Then, right before he was carried into the dugout, Lowenstein sat up and raised both arms, hands clenched. The crowd roared, and he plopped back down.

CATCH THIS: Shortstop Luis Aparicio (1963-67) had an interesting pregame responsibility. When the team was on the road, and took the bus from the hotel to the ballpark, it was his job to look out of the window when stopped at stoplights. If there were any attractive ladies in view, it was his duty to alert the players. A bus, being up so high, after all, provides a special vantage point.

A STRIKING IDEA: Outfielder Willie Tasby (1958-60) was supposed to be a great prospect but he never panned out. One day there was chance of a thunderstorm at the ballpark, so Tasby took off his shoes and headed out to center field in his stockings. He thought his spikes would attract lightning.

BIRD OF A DIFFERENT FEATHER: Of all the current Birds, sideburned outfielder Brady Anderson is the strangest. "He marches to the beat of his own drummer," O's assistant PR director Bill Stetka said. "He comes across as this California surfer-dude, but he's very dedicated to working out. He dates models and tennis players and he's very intelligent and his mind is always working. If he hears a song on the radio, he'll play

'Name That Tune' with you and you have to beat him.

"He knows the history of the game. He'll come up here (to the Orioles offices in the warehouse), sit down with a Baseball Encyclopedia and study it."

MOE WAS NO SCHMOE: The all-time great Orioles iconoclast, however, remains Moe Drabowsky, the "Clown Prince" of the Orioles from 1966-68 and 1970. Born in Poland, Drabowsky was best-remembered for his imaginative clubhouse stunts, but he contributed to Baltimore's on-field success as well. His shining moment came in the 1966 World Series, when he pitched 6 $2/3$ innings of one-hit relief.

MOE DRABOWSKY

Like Brady Anderson, Drabowsky had a quick mind. But even though he earned an economics degree from Trinity College, Drabowsky wasn't too educated to enjoy a good practical joke. He used to hang rubber snakes in players' uniforms before games. When that became passé, he graduated to real, live snakes in the clubhouse. That trick so spooked teammates Luis Aparicio and Paul Blair that they opted to dress in the hallway instead ... even when that cement floor was cold.

"The first time I met Moe Drabowsky was at one of Larry McTague's restaurants in New York," said Jay Johnstone, one of baseball's all-time nut cases. "Larry said, 'Jay, I'd like you to meet Moe Drabowsky.' With that, Moe dropped his cocktail glass and reached out to shake my hand. I mean, it shattered all over the floor and he didn't even blink an eye. I knew right away this was my kind of guy."

Drabowsky was the master of the hotfoot. That alone was kind of basic, obligatory stuff, but he was able to elevate that old trick to legendary status by giving one to the almighty baseball commissioner himself, Bowie Kuhn, during the 1970 World Series title celebration.

ANOTHER PARTICULARLY HILARIOUS STUNT: Drabowsky used to find out the phone number of the opposing team's bullpen, call them and tell so-and-so to "start warming up."

Drabowsky pulled his stunts to ease the pressures of a professional relief pitcher. But he made people laugh in the process. According to Ted Patterson's book, *The Baltimore Orioles: 40 Years of Magic from 33rd St. to Camden Yards*, Drabowsky received a postcard from an 11-year old fan who wrote: "Baseball needs more nuts like you."

HE GOT HIMSELF IN A STICKY SITUATION: Not all of the nuts were ballplayers. Sometimes the nuttiest things happened to fans; so nutty, in fact, that they got covered in them.

According to an anecdote by Craig Neff in the May 23, 1988 issue of *Sports Illustrated*, it occurred during the season of Baltimore's record-breaking streak for season-opening ineptitude. The Orioles started the season with 21 consecutive losses, and it was in the midst of that run when Mike Filippelli, a morning disc jockey at Ocean City, Md., station WWTR-FM and lifelong O's booster, made a bet with broadcast partner Vince Edwards. Filippelli predicted, on the air, that the Baltimore streak would not reach 13, then the season-opening record. The two deejays let listeners choose the stakes.

Turns out that wasn't such a good idea for Filippelli. The Orioles, of course, kept on losing, and Filippelli had to pay up. First he had to crawl and walk a 6.2 mile stretch of Maryland's Coastal Highway, which took four hours.

That was the easy part.

Wrote Neff: "Next he went to the Ocean Plaza Mall, where, dressed in an Orioles jersey and helmet, he sat down in a plastic kiddie pool and let Edwards pour 30 gallons of chocolate syrup over him. While Edwards watched and gloated, mall patrons decorated Filippelli with cherries, pineapple, jimmies, nuts and whipped cream – the works. 'After two hours of that, I can make it through a season of humiliation with the Orioles,' says Filippelli, adding, 'It was something not to tell my grandchildren about.' "

He doesn't have to now. They can read about it in this book.

BUT HE LEFT THE CREAM CHEESE ALONE: Moe Drabowsky's prankster spirit lives on today with the Orioles public relations staff.

A beat writer from Pennsylvania, trying to get on the good side of then-Orioles manager Davey Johnson, left a bag of fresh bagels on Johnson's desk with a schmoozing note. Orioles PR director John Maroon – who certainly didn't want any problems with favoritism escalating among members of the media – happened by Johnson's office and noticed the bag and note.

Before Johnson arrived, Maroon took a bite out of each bagel and put them back in the sack.

A VIEW FROM THE INSIDE: Orioles assistant PR director Bill Stetka has spent his life studying the Orioles from just about every vantage point: As a fan growing up in Baltimore, where he lived so close to Memorial Stadium he could leave the house by 7:30 p.m., purchase a ticket and be sitting in his seat by the 8 p.m. opening pitch; as a sportswriter for the Baltimore News-American, he covered the team as an objective observer; then he was the ballclub's official scorer for three years; and now, as assistant to public relations director John Maroon, he's an Orioles employee, servicing the media and promoting the club. The best thing about his current post, he says, is "being on the inside and seeing how the whole thing operates."

The good news is you get to find out all kinds of inside scoops. The bad news is you can't tell them to anybody.

On Dec. 21, 1995, the Orioles signed All-Star free agent Roberto Alomar to a three-year contract. What most people didn't know was that the club also nearly signed star pitcher David Cone. Owner Peter Angelos had given new general manager Pat Gillick approval to sign both players if it was financially feasible. Prior to the signing, Maroon and Stetka didn't know what was going to happen, so they prepared for each scenario. They collected notes and put together a press release for an Alomar signing; a release for a Cone signing; and a release for a Cone AND Alomar signing.

When a team signs or trades for a new player, standard press conference procedure calls for that player to don his new club's cap and to hold up a new jersey with his name sewn on the back. The Orioles prepared jerseys for both Alomar and Cone. When Cone instead decided to re-sign with New York, Stetka stowed that jersey in his office closet. Baltimore signed Alomar and held the press conference for him.

A month later Stetka's closet door happened to be open when a sportswriter sauntered in. The writer saw the jersey with C-O-N-E stitched over the back shoulders and said, "What's up with THAT?" Said Stetka, "I don't think anybody realized how close we were to signing David Cone."

DEJA VU?   Maybe the Orioles' PR staff knows even more than we think. On page 17 of the team's 1997 Information and Record Book, the PR staff printed a photo of pitching coach Ray Miller on the divider page titled "Managers and Coaches." But Davey Johnson was the team's manager at the time. Miller was hired as manager after Johnson resigned November 5, 1997.

CAN YOU TOP THIS?   Of all the Orioles pranks, perhaps the grandest one of them all began in 1997.
What started off as the simplest of stunts has escalated to global proportions.

One day Orioles PR director John Maroon took the nameplate of administrative assistant Jennifer Steier and flipped it upside down. When Steier discovered the culprit, she took Maroon's nameplate and replaced it with assistant Bill Stetka's. Soon the two became embroiled in a battle of one-upmanship. A game of inter-office hide-and-seek ensued.

When that got old, Maroon graduated to Camden Yards, taping her name plate to a club-level advertisement sign. Steier had to walk along the front row and lean over, feeling around, while Maroon borrowed a telephoto lens and, from the field, photographed her search.

Maroon's nameplate soon ended up taped to Camden Yards' scoreboard support; Steier had the cameras of Home Team Sports, a regional TV Network, capture it during a live broadcast.

The battle became the talk of the Warehouse. Joe Foss, the Orioles' vice chairman of business and finance, wanted to get involved in the action. It didn't take long. During a road trip to Texas, Home Team Sports was coming out of a commercial break and showed Stetka talking with assistant general manager Pat Gillick in the press box. In front of them was the nameplate of Joe Foss.

But Foss was well-connected. He arranged with President Bill Clinton's support staff to tape not one but FIVE nameplates to the podium of the White House press room.

"If you want this to continue," Foss said, "you're going to have to top the White House."

Two days later the boys in PR were busy trying to figure out their next step.

	1	2	3	4	5	6	7	8	9	F
Visitor	0	0	0	0	0	0	0	0	0	
Orioles	1	1	1	1	1	1	1	1	1	

NINTH INNING
Postseason memories

"Once an Oriole, always an Oriole." – Don Baylor, Colorado Rockies manager.

A club can have all the off-the-field fun imaginable. It can have star players. It can have a wonderful stadium. It can have rabid fans (just ask the Chicago Cubs). But what really sets a franchise apart from the rest, is its ability – or inability – to win (just ask the Chicago Cubs).

The Baltimore Orioles win. From 1966 to 1983 the O's won three world championships (1966, 1970, 1983), six pennants (1969, '71, '79) and eight division titles (1973, '74). In 1996 they earned a trip to the American League playoffs, and in 1997 they compiled the best record in the American League (98-64, a winning percentage of .605) and second-best in baseball behind the Atlanta Braves. Not bad for a team that started playing baseball by the Chesapeake Bay in 1954.

FIRST TASTE OF GLORY: Baltimore's first season of glory came in 1966, the same year the Supreme's "You Can't Hurry Love" and Donovan's "Sunshine Superman" topped the charts, miniskirts were in fashion, and Jacqueline Susann published the controversial novel *Valley of the Dolls*.

According to *Baseball Weekly's* Bill Koenig, the secret to Baltimore's first World Series title was found in just one afternoon.

Camden Yards was ready for the 1997 playoffs.

The results were dramatic: The O's put together 33 consecutive innings and swept the Los Angeles Dodgers in four games.

The secret? "Outside fastballs," catcher Andy Etchebarren told Koenig. "We kept it on the outside part of the plate. It was their weakness, at least in that Series."

But the Orioles came across this interesting bit of information accidentally. Opening game starter Dave McNally inexplicably lost his control in the third inning and manager Hank Bauer replaced him with Moe Drabowsky. Drabowsky threw 6 $2/3$ innings of long relief, striking out 11 Dodgers.

"He did it by throwing 95% fastballs on the outside part of the plate," Etchebarren told Koenig. "That was the key to the entire Series. After the game, I went in and told Hank to throw out the scouting report and throw as many outside fastballs as we could until they could hit them." The Dodgers never got another run in the series and hit .142.

"Jim Palmer was a fastball pitcher anyway and he shut them out the next day," Etchebarren told Koenig. "Wally Bunker had two good fastballs – a sinker and a rising fastball. And McNally came back in Game Four with 80% fastballs, way out of his normal range.

"(That series is) still the greatest moment in my life. We broke camp that year with three rookies up the middle -- myself behind the plate, Davey (Johnson, the former O's manager) at second and Paul Blair in center field. We got a lot of criticism for that, people saying we couldn't win with three rookies."

The Orioles finished 97-63, winning their first American League pennant since moving from St. Louis in 1954. Newcomer Frank Robinson won the Triple Crown, hitting .316 with 49 home runs and 122 RBI.

Frank Robinson, third baseman Brooks Robinson and first baseman Boog Powell gave the Orioles their first trio of 100-RBI men in the same season. Powell hit .287 with 34 home runs and 109 RBI, while Brooks hit .269 with 23 home runs and 100 RBI. Rookie Curt Blefary added 23 homers.

IT TOOK A MIRACLE TO BEAT THE O'S IN 1969:   When Orioles fans think back upon the tragedies of the Sixties, several things come to mind: The Kennedy assassinations, the tragic death of Martin Luther King, Vietnam – and losing the World Series to the Mets.

Former Manager Davey Johnson, greeting Seattle manager Lou Piniella, are playoff veterans as both players and skippers.

Ask a diehard O's fan what was the worst day of his or her life, and they're likely to say Oct. 15, 1969. It was Game Four of the World Series, and the Mets had won Game Three the day before thanks to two amazing catches by center fielder Tommy Agee. New York led the Series two games to one.

In the ninth inning, with the score tied, Brooks Robinson lined the ball to right field. Ron Swoboda, not known for his fielding prowess, dove for it. Not a smart play; if the ball got past him, the winning run would have been in scoring position. But he dove for it anyway – and made the catch. The irony of it all was that Swoboda was from Baltimore.

The Mets went on to win 2-1 in the 10th inning.

What made the loss more painful was that it came from a New York team. In January, the Jets had upset the Baltimore Colts in Super Bowl III. And that spring, the New York Knicks bounced the Baltimore Bullets from the NBA playoffs.

THE BROOKS SERIES (1970):   The Orioles beat the Reds four games to one in 1970, thanks to the legendary glove work of third baseman Brooks Robinson. The O's fans throughout Baltimore who couldn't get tickets would gather at corner taverns in anticipation of what great feat Robinson would perform that night. "I've never seen a guy dominate a series from a defensive position like Brooks," writer John Hunt said. "You just don't see things like that anymore."

BEST DOESN'T ALWAYS WIN (1971):   Most observers regarded the Orioles as the best team in baseball in 1971, and they were red-hot going into the World Series. Baltimore had won its last 11 regular season games to finish 101-57, swept the Oakland A's in the playoffs and won the first two games of the World Series against Pittsburgh. But Steve Blass beat the O's 5-1 with a three-hitter in Game Three, and Roberto Clemente's Pirates won three of the next four games to take the title.

Blass won two games in the series, striking out 13 and walking just four. And he credited O's manager Earl Weaver for some of his success. In Game Seven, Blass was on the mound when Weaver ran out yelling "Rule 8.01!" He claimed Blass was lining up improperly on the rubber in his stretch because his left heel was off to the first base side. "It was a Kmart psyche job," Blass told *Baseball Weekly's* Bill Koenig. "Earl didn't realize he was pumping me up with his antics. I still thank him every time I see him."

WE ARE UN-HAPPY (1979):   The Orioles stayed at Pittsburgh's venerable William Penn Hotel during the 1979 World Series, and Baltimore manager Earl Weaver wasn't too fond of it. "I think William Penn may have been named after the hotel, rather than the other way around," he said.

It was one of those Series. The "We Are Family" Pittsburgh Pirates defeated the O's in seven games, after Baltimore had taken three-games-to-one lead.

ALMOST (1982):   Although Baltimore didn't make the playoffs in 1982, it provided its fans with one of the most memorable weekends of competition ever. The Orioles won 17 of 18 games from Aug. 20-Sept 7, but with five games left they were still four games out. They beat Detroit 6-5 on Sept. 30, and going into the season's final series, against the first-place Milwaukee Brewers, the O's were three games out with four to play. A weekend sweep would give them the AL East title.

Baltimore took the Oct. 1 doubleheader by scores of 8-3 and 7-1 to cut the lead to one game. On Oct. 2 the O's won again, this time 11-3. Going into the last day of the regular season, the two teams were even at 94-67.

"The final weekend of the 1982 was some of the best baseball I've ever seen," said *Baseball Weekly* senior writer Bill Koenig. "Friday and Saturday were just incredible. The place was electric."

The O's had their ace, Jim Palmer, on the mound. Milwaukee countered with Don Sutton, elected into the Hall of Fame in 1998. Earl Weaver had announced his retirement (he would later come out of retirement to coach two more years). Baltimore had the momentum and the emotion.

But the Brewers' Robin Yount hit two home runs and a triple and Sutton, who had been traded to Milwaukee Aug. 30, held the O's to two runs. Even though Milwaukee won 10-2 and the Orioles lost the pennant, the fans gave Weaver a lengthy standing ovation.

THE AMTRAK SERIES (1983):   The Orioles beat Philadelphia in five games as Rick Dempsey was named Series MVP.

According to *Sports Illustrated*, Dempsey went by the nickname "Moe" during the Series, because he was one of the O's "Three Stooges" that came up in the batting order behind John Lowenstein. Rich Dauer was "Larry" and Todd Cruz was "Curly." The three had a combined batting average of .228 during the season.

Ken Singleton gave The Stooges their name. At the end of the season, according to *SI*, he had said he was proud of his 85 RBI "especially with the Three Stooges in the lineup." Singleton said the trio took offense to his comment initially, but then they came around and started calling each other by their Stooges nickname.

Dempsey said he was "Moe" because he was the most intelligent of the three. Cruz was "Curly" because that was his favorite Stooge – and he had a heckuva back-step. Pitcher Mike Boddicker wanted to get in on the act and asked if he could be "Shemp," the Stooge who replaced Curly, because he pinch-hit for Cruz and got an RBI. Singleton said no, because he made too much contact.

According to *Sports Illustrated's* Jerry Kirshenbaum, the victorious Orioles were on their bus riding home after their fifth-game victory over the Phillies. "As the bus reached the Delaware line on Interstate 95, the driver announced on the intercom: 'We have just left Pennsylvania, home of the world-champion Philadelphia ...' There was a long pause before the driver finished the sentence: '.. 76ers.' "

1996: The Orioles might have made it to the 1996 World Series if not for 12-year old Yankees fan Jeffrey Maier. It was Oct. 9, game one of the ALCS in Yankee Stadium. New York shortstop Derek Jeter hit a long fly ball to right field. Baltimore outfielder Tony Tarasco settled under it when Maier stuck out his glove and deflected the ball into the stands. It should have been ruled fan interference, but umpire Richie Garcia signaled that it was a game-tying home run. The Yankees went on to win 5-4 in 11 innings and eventually took the series. The next day, the New York Post headline read:

"ANGEL IN THE OUTFIELD"
Schoolboy helps snatch victory from jaws of defeat

"If it was a home run for us, George Steinbrenner would have Maier on the Throgs Neck Bridge dangling somewhere," Bobby Bonilla said.

Among the best signs spotted outside Baltimore's Camden Yards: "Spank the Yanks, the Umps and the Kid." Another read, "I HATE THAT KID."

	1	2	3	4	5	6	7	8	9	F
Visitor	0	0	0	0	0	0	0	0	0	0
Orioles	1	1	1	1	1	1	1	1	1	9

EXTRA INNINGS

"On the entrance application they asked me my church prefer-ence. I wrote, 'brick.' " – Asked to remain anonymous

A couple of the cool things about this book are its price (anybody can afford it) and its size. It fits easily into the inside pocket of a sportcoat or, albeit a little tighter, into the seat pocket of your jeans. Which means you can take it with you when you visit your favorite watering hole, and that's where this chapter comes in. It's quiz time.

We're not going to ask you anything about your church prefer-ence, but we are going to ask you lots of questions about the Orioles. After you've taken this little test, try it out on your friends. See who's the most knowledgeable Orioles fan in your group. Questions were assigned different point totals depending on their relative importance. For instance, you might be the only person who knows what kind of champagne the team drank after winning the 1983 World Series, but who really cares?

Read on, have fun, and don't cheat. Answers follow.

QUESTION ONE (3 points)
Who was the Orioles' radio voice for the inaugural year of Memorial Stadium?

QUESTION TWO (1 point; this is an easy one)
What was the team's nickname and city before it moved to Baltimore?

QUESTION THREE (4 points)
Who is Joe Codd, and what is his legacy?

QUESTION FOUR (3 points)
What is the significance of this address: 216 Emory Street, Baltimore, Md.?

QUESTION FIVE (3 points)
What early Orioles hero had a road in Baltimore County named after him?

QUESTION SIX (2 points)
How many times was the All-Star game held at Memorial Stadium?

QUESTION SEVEN (3 points)
Who hit the only ball ever to leave Memorial Stadium, and what year?

QUESTION EIGHT (1 point)
After winning the 1983 World Series in five games, what champagne did the Orioles celebrate with? And how many bottles did they use? Note: If you know this, you were either in the clubhouse, or you're one sick puppy.

QUESTION NINE (2 points)
What is the significance of the date April 6, 1979? Hint: The answer will crack you up.

QUESTION 10 (2 points)
Which Seinfeld character was a devout Orioles fan?

QUESTION 11 (3 points)
Who threw the first pitch in Camden Yards, against what batter and team?

QUESTION 12 (4 points)
What Oriole great did Roger Maris overshadow in 1961, the year he slugged a major-league record 61 home runs?

QUESTION 13 (4 points)
What pitcher notched his 20th win of the season earlier than any other Oriole?

QUESTION 14 (2 points)
What is the significance of Sunday, May 30, 1982?

QUESTION 15 (5 points)
Who replaced Cal Ripken at third base in the second game of a doubleheader the day before Ripken began his streak?

QUESTION 16 (1 point)
What kind of grass makes up the field at Camden Yards?

QUESTION 17 (3 points)
What pitcher has lost more games to the Orioles than anyone else?

QUESTION 18 (3 points)
And what pitcher has beaten them more than anyone else?

QUESTION 19 (2 points)
Who are the only two Orioles to have ever hit for the cycle? Hint: They both played the same position.

QUESTION 20 (3 points)
Every aisle seat in Camden Yards bears an extra feature. What is it?

QUESTION 21 (4 points)
In 1970 eight Orioles were selected for the All-Star game. Name them.

QUESTION 22 (1 point)
Has Baltimore ever had a player named Budweiser?

QUESTION 23 (3 points)
Who hit over 20 home runs and stole over 20 bases for the Orioles during the 1976 season?

QUESTION 24 (1 point)
What Oriole was named 1973 AL Rookie of the Year?

QUESTION 25 (2 points)
Who was the first modern Oriole to be inducted into the Baseball Hall of Fame? Hint: He was the wrong kind of bird.

ANSWERS

1. Hall-of-Famer Ernie Harwell. He was the voice of the Orioles from 1954-59. Hall-of-Famer Chuck Thompson. did Orioles games in 1955-56 and again from 1962-87. Both men are Ford C. Frick Award winners.

2. The St. Louis Browns.

3. A member of the Orioles' ticket office staff. He is the only person to be with the Baltimore organization since its inception in 1954.

4. Sure, it's just a long fly ball from Camden Yards. But the correct answer: The birthplace of the biggest legend in baseball history, Babe Ruth.

5. Catcher Gus Triandos, who played for Baltimore from 1955-62.

6. Once, in 1958.

7. Frank Robinson, 1966. A flag that said simply, "HERE" marked the spot. No mention of Robinson, his jersey number, the home run, nothing. And isn't that the ultimate tribute?

8. In the postgame madness, the Orioles washed down 240 bottles of Great Western Extra Dry.

9. It was the day the Oriole Bird was hatched out of a giant egg at Memorial Stadium and became the team's official mascot.

10. Elaine Benes (Julia Louis-Dreyfus); in the series she hailed from Towson, Md.

11. Rick Sutcliffe to Kenny Lofton of the Indians.

12. First baseman Jim Gentile, who hit .302 with 46 homers and 141 RBI that same year.

13. Steve Stone, who picked it up on Aug. 19, 1980. He went 25-7 that season.

14. It was the day Cal Ripken began his consecutive-games streak.

15. Floyd Rayford, a third baseman/catcher who played for the Orioles in 1980, '82 and '84-87.

16. Three strains of Kentucky Blue Grass. Midnight, Eclipse and

Touchdown (Midnight is the darker of the three).

17. Jim "Catfish" Hunter lost to Baltimore 24 times, including eight of his last 11 decisions against them from 1976-79. But he's also the second-biggest winner ever against the O's, beating them 26 times.

18. Hall of Famer Whitey Ford of the New York Yankees posted a 30-16 record against Baltimore.

19. Two legends: Brooks Robinson July 15, 1960, against the Chicago White Sox, five hits, including two singles. And Cal Ripken, May 6, 1984, vs. Texas.

20. A reproduction of the 100-year logo used by the Baltimore Orioles of the 1890s, a National League team that won consecutive pennants in 1894-95-96.

21. Starting pitcher Jim Palmer, starting outfielder Frank Robinson, starting first baseman Boog Powell, starting second baseman Dave Johnson, third baseman Brooks Robinson, pitchers Mike Cuellar and Dave McNally (both of whom did not play), and manager Earl Weaver.

22. No, but they had a player named Brideweser. Jim played for the O's from 1954-57.

23. Reggie Jackson hit 27 homers and stole 28 bases for the Orioles in '76. It was the only season he played for them.

24. Al Bumbry. He was inducted into the Orioles Hall of Fame in 1987.

25. Right-hander Robin Roberts, who pitched in Baltimore from 1962-65. He was inducted in 1976, receiving 87% of the vote.

SCORING SCALE

(**0-24**): Better take some more batting practice.

(**25-34**): Single. Maybe you should take this test sober next time.

(**35-44**): Double. Not bad. (You probably even know how many windows there are in the Warehouse.)

(**45-54**): Triple. (And how often they get washed.)

(**55-65**): Home run. (And with what kind of soap.)

If you scored at least 55, you are a true die-hard Orioles fan whose dream is to be cremated and have your ashes spread over the outfield grass of Camden Yards, or even better, around third base. You have scorecards you've kept from every Orioles game since 1954, your Orioles bobbing head doll is your most prized possession and you think Cal Ripken is a logical candidate for President one day – IF he ever retires from baseball.

You still love the smell of fresh-cut grass in the morning. There is nothing quite like the feeling of pounding your fist into a well-worn glove. Few things in life taste as good to you as an Esskay hot dog with yellow mustard at the ballpark. There is no more beautiful sound than the crack of a wooden bat against a thrown ball, especially when Ripken is at the plate.

And the most beautiful sight in the world is seeing your hometown players in their snow-white uniforms, trimmed in black and orange, trotting out onto the vivid green grass of Camden Yards on Opening Day.

To be an Orioles fan is to be a baseball fan. So many of the great moments and outstanding achievements and dramatic moments have involved Orioles. From the basic backdrop of Memorial Stadium to the glitz of Camden Yards, the Orioles have always been about the essence of the game. Finding an angle. Good pitching. Slick fielding. Timely hitting.

The comedian Mel Brooks once said, "It's good to be the king." And maybe he was right.

But it's even better to be an Orioles fan.

Orioles in the Hall of Fame

Robin Roberts 1976
Frank Robinson 1982
Brooks Robinson 1983
George Kell 1983
Luis Aparicio 1984
Hoyt Wilhelm 1985
Jim Palmer 1990
Reggie Jackson 1993
Earl Weaver 1996

Orioles Retired Numbers

4 - Earl Weaver
5 - Brooks Robinson
20 - Frank Robinson
22 - Jim Palmer
33 - Eddie Murray

Oriole American League Most Valuable Player Award Winners

1964 - Brooks Robinson
1966 - Frank Robinson
1970 - Boog Powell
1983 - Cal Ripken, Jr.
1991 - Cal Ripken, Jr.

Oriole Cy Young Award Winners

1969 - Mike Cuellar (tied with Denny McLain)
1973 - Jim Palmer
1975 - Jim Palmer
1976 - Jim Palmer
1979 - Mike Flanagan
1980 - Steve Stone

Manager of the Year

1989 - Frank Robinson

World Series Most Valuable Player

1966 - Frank Robinson
1970 - Brooks Robinson
1983 - Rick Dempsey

Orioles No-hitters

Hoyt Wilhelm, vs New York	9/20/58
Steve Barber / Stu Miller, vs Detroit	4/30/67 (Orioles lost the game)
Tom Phoebus, vs Boston	4/27/68
Jim Palmer, vs Oakland	8/13/69
Bob Milacki / Mike Flanagan / Mark Williamson	
/ Greg Olson, vs Oakland	7/13/91

About the Author:

Chris Colston is the assistant operations editor at *USA TODAY'S Baseball Weekly*. He has won two national writing awards, presented by the College Sports Information Directors of America. He worked 11 years as editor of the *Hokie Huddler*, Virginia Tech's official sports newspaper, and is the author of *Hokies Handbook: Stories, Stats and Stuff About Virginia Tech Football*, published in 1996. He has contributed to both the *Roanoke Times* and the *USA TODAY* Information Network. Colston, 40, lives in Reston, Virginia.